The NewComers

Austria, Finland and Sweden

Richard Hill
David Haworth

A Division of Europublic SA/NV

Published by Europublications, Division of Europublic SA/NV,
Avenue Winston Churchill 11 (box 21), B-1180 Brussels.
Tel: + 32 2 343 77 26, Fax: + 32 2 343 93 30.

Cover design : U & I Communication, Brussels

Printed in Belgium. Edition et Imprimerie, Brussels.
D/1995/6421/1   ISBN 90-74440-06-1

This book is dedicated to Melanie and Paula, also newcomers.

Contents

The
NewComers

Austria

Finland

Sweden

Introduction

Now that the European Union counts 15 fully fledged members*, an unimaginable development for the founders of the original Six over 35 years ago, the full scope and cultural complexity of the Union is hard to grasp.

It is particularly important to take stock of the three newcomers - Austria, Finland and Sweden - even as we breathlessly contemplate yet another EU extension to include the former communist countries within the next decade.

EU citizens are now supposed to know a great deal more about each other than before this unique comity was created in 1957. One might add, for good measure, **like** one another more.

Do we though? While we have certainly learned a lot about one another, the EU's size and the cultural diversity of its member states still leave us with gaps in our knowledge.

Even if we became used to the complexities of the 'Europe of the Twelve' and took many of its members' idiosyncrasies for granted (and for jokes), contrast was always a sub-theme of the way the EU was reported and discussed.

That contrast is even greater today with the three new members on the northern and eastern flanks of the old European Community.

Anyone who thinks that Austria is an extension of a cultural '*Großdeutschland*' is sadly misled and, moreover, com-

---

* incidentally bringing the EU's economy to nearly ECU 6.5 trillion GDP, the number of inhabitants to 370 million and the total area to 3.24 million km².

mitting an impropriety in the eyes of both the Austrians and the Germans.

Indeed the Republic of Austria is a complex definition in its own right, bringing together as it does the essentially central European city of Vienna and the more westernised outer reaches of Tyrol and Vorarlberg. Many Europeans are aware of Austria as a tourist attraction, but know very little else about the country and its people.

Equal, if not greater, unfamiliarity applies to the newcomers north of Brussels: Finland and Sweden. The first solecism we other Europeans make is to talk about them as 'Scandinavians' (a classification that extends only to Sweden and its independently-minded neighbour, Norway). We should be saying 'Nordics'.

The second and far greater error is to think that these countries and their peoples are essentially alike. Not so, if you happen to be a Finn or a Swede (or a Norwegian!).

Unfamiliarity is also compounded, in some cases, by indifference. "Boringly Scandinavian" is how Britain's *Sunday Times* described Nordic affairs some time ago. Auberon Waugh said much the same thing - only even more offensively - specifically about the Swedes*. Yet, why 'boring'? These countries are just as fascinating, if only by virtue of their divergence from the pundits' view of what is interesting

---

* "Sweden works, of course, in the sense that Swedes are born (in ever decreasing numbers), eat, copulate and eventually (thank God) die, without the extremes of violence or starvation which one sees in such countries as the United States of America or Ethiopia. They put up repulsive buildings and live in them, washing their almost hairless bodies with great thoroughness under the shower whenever necessary. Their conversation is so boring it makes one gasp and stretch one's eyes, and they have not had an original thought between them in the last 150 years."

or not. Such attitudes are never properly explained or justified. They are just assumed.

This overview of the EU's new members makes no such assumptions. It is written on the basis that these countries and cultures bring an important new element to the Union and should therefore be properly addressed. Not in a spirit of solemnity, but rather in one of exuberance and discovery.

Each of the three nations under review is, for most people in the member states of the 'Twelve', a bit like a distant second cousin. Their faces are familiar, we know the essential things about them like age, civil status and so on but - now we come to think of it - we don't know them that well! This book aims to fill in some of the details and, hopefully, both help and entertain the reader at the same time.

We particularly intend to show how distinctly and entertainingly different are the new Nordic arrivals. Different not only from the rest of us, but also different from one another.

History, culture and language sharply distinguish these countries from one another. For practical reasons, but also as a matter of simple respect, we should be alert to these divergences. From now on, the Baltic will be as integrated with the European ideal as the Mediterranean has been up till now. 'Midnight Sun' will become part of the cultural grammar of the enlarged EU.

For expedient reasons, this book deals with the new members in the order in which they voted in the latter part of 1994 to join the Union: Austria, Finland and Sweden. We have also a added a postscript on Norway.

In different ways and capacities we have spent long apprenticeships with and in the new member states, contacts which began years before there seemed any prospect of any of them joining the EU. Indeed, the very suggestion would have been treated as some kind of outlandish joke.

13

Yet here we are with new partners, Alpine and Nordic, with whom there is little familiarity in Brussels so far. Except in a narrowly geographical sense, these nations are no longer peripheral to Europe. But who are they? What are they really like? What can we expect from them? How do we cohabit and conduct business with these new boys on the EU block?

We have asked questions from the Alps to the tundra, and hope to provide some of the answers in what follows. If the least we can do is to persuade the reader that not all Austrians are leather-thigh-slapping types and not all Nordics are gloomy, then we will have done our job.

The
NewComers

Austria

Austria, the underestimated

T he first of our countries is the least homogeneous of the newcomers to the European Union and in this respect presents a particular challenge.

Partly as a consequence of the complex geography and the turbulent history of this part of Central Europe, with Vienna playing a dominant role in first the Habsbourg dominions and then the Austro-Hungarian Empire, the country's nine provinces betray subtle differences in orientation*.

Most roads do indeed lead to Vienna. Yet the southern provinces of Carinthia and Styria look as much towards their southern neighbours, these days Italy in particular, and display some of the lighter-hearted characteristics of the Latins; the Tyrol and Vorarlberg have strong affinities with their neighbours to the west; and Salzburg and Upper Austria, the province dominated by the industrial complex of Linz, look - sometimes slightly resentfully - over their shoulders at big brother Germany to the north and west.

It is not surprising that circumstances encourage Austria, located as it is in the centre of Central Europe, to look outwards as much as inwards. Even much of the attention in the provinces of both Burgenland and Styria is directed towards the country's troublesome neighbours to the southeast. The only thing that unites the provinces is a common dislike of the capital - a phenomenon by no means exclusive to Austria!

---

* As an English-language publication, this book uses the English spelling for placenames.

Meanwhile Vienna, a city rebuilt in the 19th century by Czech workers who then stayed to enjoy the fruits of their labours, has a strong orientation to the countries to the north and east - an orientation that has been given major impetus by the dismantling of the Iron Curtain. In fact, as recently as 1910, more than half the population of Vienna was of Czech or Hungarian origin.

So even more than with most European Union countries, the visitor to Austria is confronted with not one, but a number of cultures. The common factor is the German language - *pace* the small Croat and Slovene minority groups in the east and south. At the administrative level, Austria's provinces enjoy a certain amount of autonomy, though not to the same degree as Germany's *Länder*.

Austria is intriguing precisely because, beyond the usual clichés, it is relatively little known to outsiders.

Maybe as a consequence of the self-deprecating humour of many influential Austrians (see box, page 29), and as a hangover from the days when Vienna was the capital of a major European power, the country seems not to enjoy the reputation it deserves. Despite a well-run external information programme, the message is not getting through as it should. The minds of some foreigners are still clouded by memories of the *Anschluß*, the 1938 political union with Germany, and of more recent events. These encourage them to adopt an unduly reserved attitude to what has, in the meantime, evolved into an exemplary democracy despite the inevitable occasional failings.

Item: Austria is now one of the ten wealthiest countries in the world. On a per capita basis, its economic performance exceeds the average in the European Union, ranking fourth after Germany, Denmark and Luxembourg, and slightly ahead of France.

Item: using OECD methods of calculation, Austria has an unemployment rate of less than 4.5%. At the time of publication, this is the lowest rate in the enlarged European Union after Luxembourg.

Item: in terms of percentage of GDP (nearly 2%), Austria is investing more in environmental protection than any other country of the world. Its industries are now supplying new technologies, knowhow and equipment to the world market.

Unless arriving by plane (air travellers don't realise what they are missing), the approach for most European Unionists visiting Austria's capital is the Passau-Vienna motorway, partly a relic of the *Anschluß*. While the motorway shows signs of encroaching old age, the surrounding landscape shows plenty of evidence of a vital and extremely well-run country.

A question of identity

It is important to pause at this point and recollect the trauma that this little country of just under 8 million people has known in the course of only a few generations and a century.

There are still many Austrians alive who witnessed the collapse of the Austro-Hungarian Empire in 1918, followed by the well-intentioned but unhappy experiment of the First Republic which succumbed to a Civil War, then to the *Anschluß* and total war and, finally, the Second Republic which chose neutrality more as a political expedient than as a solemn commitment.

Having been deprived of, or lost, a clear identity, Austrians found a radical solution: to be identified as non-identifiable. This solution did them less than justice and ultimately proved to be no more than a stopgap. In the words of Otto von Habsburg, who was particularly well placed to make the remark, *"Wer nicht weiß woher er kommt, weiß nicht wohin er geht, weiß daher nicht wo er steht"* ["Anyone who doesn't know where he's coming from and doesn't know where he's going to, doesn't know where he is"].

The Second Republic also chose the sensible formula of the *Sozialpartnerschaft*, a corporatist insurance policy for peace and prosperity which, as events subsequently showed, paid dividends. Yet, as Robert Menasse says in his book 'Das Land ohne Eigenschaften', "This system, social partnership, had the effect of making all social and political contradictions and contrasts identical, so that soon [the issue of] Austria's identity meant no more than that [the idea of] a clearcut identity had become obsolete." In the words of an observer who, as a Swede, certainly understands the significance of the word, "Austria is the most corporatist state in western Europe."

Happily, there are now signs that Austrians are recovering their long-lost sense of confidence and, with it, a growing sense of identity. The latter is still to some extent an arbitrary one, and will be argued about for a long time to come, but it fills a gap. Essentially, it means being Austrian and proud of it. Comparing the younger generation of Austrians with their elders, Friedrich Torberg remarked: "When you say Austria, they know what you mean and when they identify themselves with this Austria, they know why."

Thanks to the legitimising influence of a Second Republic that, 40 years on, can be said - unlike its predecessor - to have withstood the test of time, Austria now feels itself to be *europareif* [ready for Europe] and capable of standing on its feet without the need for identification with a *deutschsprachige Raum*, a German-speaking zone.

As Austrians say, the *Anschluß* and WWII eventually taught them that, whatever they may be, they are not German.

But it took time. Even in 1956, 46 per cent of the population considered that the Austrians belonged to the *Deutsche Volk*. But recent opinion polls show that 90 per cent of citizens now consider their country to be a nation in its own right.

This trend has been accelerated by German engrossment with the problems of reunification with, as one result, a developing relationship with German-speaking Switzerland. Although most of the leading papers are now owned by German groups, Austrian media do not have the German 'fixation' they used to have.

There is clearly a cultural divide developing between Austria and Germany, with evidence accumulating on both sides. On the Austrian side, the northern and western provinces resent German attitudes and money, though they welcome the income from tourists. Acquisition by German retirees of land and property in the Tyrol was one of the issues in the negotiations with the European Union.

German sentiment is not dissimilar. An opinion poll conducted among undergraduates at the Gerhard Mercator university in Duisburg in late-1994 identified the two dominant characteristics of Austrians as 'arrogant' and 'nationalistic'. No doubt this has something to do with the *'anti-Piefke'** sentiment that emerged once people had made up their minds that they weren't Germans after all. Certainly, arrogance is not a characteristic that most Europeans associate with the Austrians.

The history of Austria is poorly mirrored in the physical and geographical reality of Austria today - a somewhat arbit-

---

* *Piefke*, the name used to describe a typical Berliner, was usurped first to describe all Prussians and then, by the Austrians, to describe all Germans.

rary rump of provinces left over from the Austro-Hungarian Empire with a 'head' that is really far too big for the body (1.5 million people live in Vienna out of this population of less than 8 million).

Moreover, this 'head' carries in it the collective memories of past glories that will never die, and rightly so. When the Empire collapsed in 1918, Vienna capitulated politically but was still the cultural capital *par excellence* of Central Europe. There is no need to remind the reader how much of the best in 20th century European music, art, architecture and philosophy came from Vienna, capping the cultural achievements of the previous two centuries.

These achievements still resonate today. In the words of American writer Bill Bryson, talking about Vienna, "the same impulse that leads people to preserve the past in their cities leads them also to preserve it in their hearts." But then he adds, spitefully and rather inaccurately, "no one clings to former glories as the Austrians do, and since these former glories include one of the most distasteful interludes in history, this is not their most attractive feature." If he means the *Hitlerzeit*, well, Austrians don't have much interest in talking about it and, if he means the Austro-Hungarian Empire, was it such a "distasteful interlude"?

Living down the past

Yet two not-so-savoury matters affecting Austria's image need to be dealt with at this early stage: the issues of corruption and anti-semitism.

A slew of scandals hit the country some years ago: illegal arms deals, the case of a sabotaged ship, kickbacks from the long drawn-out construction of the Vienna general hospital, and the adulterated wine scandal. Although most Western European countries have surpassed themselves in the meantime in following this example, such is the hypocrisy of others that the taint remains.

In reality, Austria has drawn its conclusions from these experiences and a rigorous cleanup has been effected in the areas concerned. The wine industry now operates, for example, to a 25-point code which it claims is the strictest in Europe.

The political principle of *Sozialpartnerschaft* [social partnership] on which the Second Republic is based - and which has helped keep the country on a steady course since WWII, with very few industrial disputes - has been accompanied by the practice of *Proporz*: jobs for the boys, a party-political carve-up like the *lottizazione* practised by the Italians. As one political observer put it, "the social partnership made corruption legal."

Further opportunities for nest-feathering were offered by the creeping nationalisation of industry in post-WWII years, when government collected a flock of big 'lame ducks'. Politics and money got hopelessly entangled for a while, though there was little evidence of criminal behaviour.

The present privatisation drive is eliminating that particular temptation and there are signs that, with increasing public criticism of the system (fuelled by the populist strictures of Jörg Haider), *Proporz* is on the wane. Temporarily, though, the reemergence of a coalition government has given the system a new lease of life and, with accession to the European Union, the government parties lost no time in proposing lists of suitable candidates for the top jobs in Brussels.

As Austrians will readily point out, there are always opportunities for mutual backscratching in a country where nearly 20 per cent of its most influential inhabitants are crowded into a single city. To quote the old saying which combines folk wisdom with the appropriate touch of Austrian deference, *"Mit dem Hut in der Hand kommt man durch das ganze Land"* ["With your hat in your hand you make your way across the land"].

As for the charge of anti-semitism, this is not an easy one to dismiss. The record is there - and is reinforced by recent events in public and political life. In her book 'Europeans' Jane Kramer notes that polls repeatedly show that about 70 per cent of Austrians do not like Jews, a little over 20 per cent actively loathe them and not quite one-tenth find them so repulsive that they are 'physically revolted in a Jew's presence'. A public opinion poll in the late-80s found that nearly 40 per cent of respondents thought the Jews partly responsible for what happened to them during WWII...

Talk to educated Austrians and they concede that there is latent anti-semitism abroad in the land. In the words of a senior government official, "there is a tendency to make judgments on racial grounds" The phenomenon is most evident, for reasons that are hard to explain, in the southern-most provinces of Styria and Carinthia. One theory is that memories of an abortive attempt in 1923 by the Kingdom of Yugoslavia to annexe part of the area, where there is an important Slovene minority, still feeds fears of a Slav takeover among the German-speaking majority.

Certainly anti-semitism can be traced a long way back in the history of the Habsburg empire. The very successful Jewish community was evicted from Vienna on two occasions and only allowed back because state finances and organisation were close to collapse. Things improved during the reign of the Empress Maria-Theresia and, even more significantly, under her son Josef II who, in 1782, promulgated a Patent of Tolerance that set new criteria for the constitutional rights of the Jewish community throughout the empire. Many were enrolled into government service, others were elevated to the ranks of nobility.

This 'revolution from above' ensured the reintegration of the Jewish community and contributed massively to the blossoming of Vienna as a cultural centre in the last two centuries

In the words of the Austrian Jewish author Stefan Zweig (who committed suicide in Brazilian exile, in despair at the Nazi's desecration of what he considered "the spiritual heart of Europe"): "Immeasurable is the share of Viennese culture the Jewish bourgeoisie has contributed by its helping and sponsoring involvement... nine-tenths of what the world celebrated as Viennese culture of the nineteenth century was a culture promoted, nurtured or in some cases even created by Viennese Jewry... There was no place where it was easier to be a European." Eminent members of this community, in addition to Stefan Zweig, included Gustav Mahler, Hugo von Hofmannsthal, Arthur Schnitzler and, of course, Siegmund Freud.

Despite recent attempts by public figures to put the record right, the older generation of Austrians, while all too aware of skeletons in the cupboard, understandably shows some reluctance to face up to the country's collective past (a reluctance that is by no means shared by some of the country's most eminent thinkers and writers*). There is a visceral rejection of public or foreign criticism of any kind. In the words of an Austrian expatriate who has returned to Vienna after a lifetime in the United States, "even gentle criticism challenges their whole existence." *Nestbeschmutzen* [fouling your nest], or telling things the way they really were, is still frowned upon by the older generation.

This hypersensitivity is understandable in the face of the often mindless and ill-informed criticism of the Austrians, and particularly the Viennese, by educated foreigners who should

---

* There is also a tradition of writers and sociologists - Friedrich Heer, Erwin Ringel, Hans-Georg Behr and Robert Menasse among many others - who use something little short of satirical shock therapy to make their compatriots sit up and think. They say the sort of things that, said by most other Europeans to their fellow-countryfolk, would start a riot...

know better or should at least take the trouble to find out what they are like and why. We are dealing, in some instances, with deliberate character assassination. Of course, some foreign intellectuals are put off by the equally mindless simplicity of *The Sound of Music*...

This same Austrian expatriate found out, however, that when the past is discussed reasonably and patiently with individual members of the older generation, there is a willingness to look at the facts and draw conclusions. As for the younger generation, they are not bothered with what happened 50 years ago, and the more educated ones are delightfully free of racial prejudice.

It remains to be seen whether Jörg Haider, the populist head of Austria's Freedom Party (FPÖ, which now diplomatically stands for *Freiheitliche Partei Österreichs*), succeeds in playing on the often provincial prejudices of angry working people and worried pensioners, and ends up with a majority in parliament.

Self-deprecating and bitter-sweet

Austrian - more specifically, Viennese - humour is often self-deprecating, but always has a bitter-sweet twist in the tail. Here are some of the better-known examples:

"The situation in Germany is serious but not hopeless: the situation in Austria is hopeless but not serious."

"We're clever people. We turned Hitler into a German and Beethoven into an Austrian."

"In July 1976 Vienna's finest bridge over the Danube, the *Reichsbrücke*, fell into the water. This produced the following exchange between a journalist and the mayor:

Journalist: 'How could this possibly have happened?'
Mayor: 'I've really no idea!'
Journalist: 'But don't you have any maintenance procedures?'
Mayor: 'Of course we do - for all our bridges!'
Journalist: 'But what does this mean?'
Mayor: 'We count them once every year!'"

"Standing on a street corner, Seppl and Rudl observe a group of long-distance runners.

'Why are they running like that?', asks Seppl.
'They're competing in a marathon', replies Rudl.
'But what are they competing for?', persists Seppl.
'The one who finishes first gets a prize', replies Rudl, patiently.
'OK', says Seppl, 'so why are the others competing...?'"

The glories and the agonies

No European country has quite as long and convoluted a history as Austria. But this is not the place to recount the complexities of a role on the world stage that lasted over one thousand years - even if it was more a matter of marriages arranged, lands won and battles lost than anything else. The history books relating the glories and agonies of the Habsburg dynasty and the Austro-Hungarian Empire have done their job.

But it is worth taking a brief look at events both before and after. Inevitably, less is written about the so-called 'Dark Ages' leading up to the year 996 when the infant Austria - an area east of the river Enns and south of the Danube, christened Ostarrichi, 'the Empire in the East' - was granted in permanence by the Holy Roman Emperor Otto III to the house of Babenberg at the start of this turbulent millenium.

There are three events that deserve mention here. The first was the appearance in the area from the 6th century, at the height of the *Völkerwanderung* from the east, of a tribe known as the Bajuvars, the Bavarians of today. Farming people, they settled and were then encouraged by the local lords to defend this area - successfully - against the incursions of the Slavs and Avars who followed them.

Genetically and linguistically, there are strong links between the Bavarians and the Austrians of today. Yet, depending on the area concerned, the latter can also claim a significant admixture of Czech, Slovene, Croat, Hungarian, German, Italian, Celtic, Nordic, Roman and even Illyrian blood.

Also significant is the presence in the easternmost province of Vorarlberg of a people of Swabian stock, historically known as the Alemanni, who arrived there via the Valais area of Switzerland (stopping finally at the river Lech) and who today still speak a dialect which bears similarities to Swabian and Swiss German.

A second event of a relatively minor nature, but with considerable significance for the future of this part of Europe, was the Bavarian Duchy's establishment, in the mid-8th century, of a protectorate over the Slavs on its eastern border. This led in time to the division between the south Slavs of the Balkans and the other Slavic tribes to the north.

The third and major pre-Habsburg event was the decision by the Frankish Emperor Charlemagne, in the year 790, to establish a markgravate designated the Carolingian *Ostmark* ['Eastern March'] between the Enns, Raab and Drau rivers. Despite a defeat at the hands of the roving Magyars at the end of the 9th century, the Ostmark just survived and laid the foundation for the political entity, Ostarrichi, that was to emerge two hundred years later in 996.

The recent past

Making a thousand-year 'fast forward' to the 20th century, it may be helpful to outline very briefly the events that followed the collapse of the Austro-Hungarian Empire.

The very first thing that happened in 1918 was that, one day after the abdication of the last Austrian Emperor, the Nationalrat, the legislative body in Vienna, declared the establishment of a 'Germano-Austrian Republic' and voted to have this western vestige of the Empire unite with Germany - only to have the Allies, not surprisingly, veto the idea.

This was followed by the bitter loss, coming on top of everything else, of the German-speaking South Tyrol to Italy and the Sudetenland to the new Czechoslovakia. An abortive attempt by the Tyrolese to create a republic of their own in 1919 - a move that was also vetoed by the Allies, who were determined to salvage something from the wreckage of the old Empire - was followed by an equally abortive referendum in Vorarlberg, whose inhabitants wanted to merge with Switzerland. The Swiss, despite the evident ethnic links, turned them down!

Austrian nerves were further shaken by an attempt by the new Kingdom of Yugoslavia to annexe forcibly those areas of Carinthia with sizeable Slovene minorities, a dispute that was resolved after a referendum the following year in Austria's favour. The only real sweetener in this very troubled period was the inclusion of what at the time was called 'West Hungary', today's Burgenland, in the new state.

As Georges Clémenceau said in 1918, *"l'Autriche, c'est ce qui reste..."* ["Austria, that's what's left over"].

This First Republic - a 'shot in the dark' when set against the country's imperial past and a political experiment that Austrians, with typical pathos, came to call "the state that no one wanted" - started off well enough despite the uncertainty, the poverty and the troublesome times. But, as the world economy stagnated, sagged and slumped, attitudes polarised and militant groups appeared on both sides.

Exacerbated by the recession and record unemployment rates, the political situation deteriorated rapidly. Desperate times encouraged drastic measures. In 1933 Chancellor Dollfuss dissolved parliament and established an authoritarian and corporatist regime, the ill-famed *Ständestaat*. The result in 1934 was civil war, heralding what was to happen in Spain two years later.

From this point on into the late-1930s, Austria reentered international history with the *Anschluß* and the country's active participation in the Second World War. Yet there were many Austrians who saw their hopes buried with the First Republic and mourned the collapse of an experiment that could have shown the way to the rest of the world.

On 27 April 1945, in a spirit of 'never again', Social Democrat Karl Renner's provisional government declared Austria's independence in accord with the Allies' Moscow Declaration of 1943. Ten years later, in May 1955, Austria signed the *Staatsvertrag* [State Treaty] with the four Allied powers: this terminated the presence of the occupying forces and established full sovereignty for the country. In October, the Second Republic declared Austria's permanent neutrality.

Under the impetus of Socialist Chancellor Bruno Kreisky - ironically one of the surviving members of Vienna's Jewish population - Austria gracefully accepted its fate as one of Europe's also-rans and adopted the role of a *'liebliches, gemütliches Land'*.

Finding a vocation

From even a bald outline of recent history like this, it must be evident that there was inevitably, and still is, much agonising by ordinary Austrians over the country's identity. This may owe something to the fact that, in the opinion of Friedrich Heer, "no historico-political entity has ever been so profoundly influenced from the outside as has Austria."

The problem has always been there. Even at the height of the Habsburg Empire, Austria was still essentially a peasant society cohabiting in the eastern and southern provinces with Hungarians and Slavs, and ruled by total strangers - the seat of the Habsburgs being in Switzerland.

The situation was exacerbated from the 16th century onwards by the dislocating effects of the Counter-Reformation

- a particularly single-minded affair managed, as always very astutely, by the Jesuits who used baroque architecture, pageantry and theatrical *divertissements* to seduce the populace. The infant protestant community, which saw Lutheranism not just as a faith but as the vector of German cultural values, found itself in opposition to the traditionalists, creating a dichotomy which did nothing to hasten the emergence of a true Austrian identity.

According to the historian and writer Friedrich Heer, the only symptoms of a genuine but anonymous Austrian sense of nationality emerged during the crises in the Empire's history, notably the wars with the Turks and the resistance to Napoleon.

In more recent times Austria has twice been abruptly distanced from what its people might, reasonably or otherwise, have regarded as their legitimate geopolitical vocation - first in 1918 when the country was stripped of most of its Empire, secondly in 1945 when a temporary and uncomfortable sejourn *'im großdeutschen Haus'* came to a sudden and painful conclusion.

These historical trauma, in the opinion of Anton Pelinka, delayed the emergence of a mature civil society, a process that was impeded also by ethnic diversity. The country stood on the sidelines during the Industrial Revolution, with developments taking place in the Ruhr to the north and in the Czech lands to the north.

Until the collapse of the Austro-Hungarian Empire in 1918, Austria remained essentially a feudal society, the "bourgeois-led revolution" of 1848 having been successfully crushed by Metternich.

A social partnership

"**A**ustria is a democratic republic. Its law emanates from the people." So runs Article 1 of the Austrian constitution. Parliament has two houses: the *Nationalrat*, with 183 members who are elected directly, and the *Bundesrat*, whose present 63 members are nominated by the provincial assemblies of the nine federal states. Draft laws supported by a minimum of 100,000 registered voters can be put to the *Nationalrat* for ratification.

The President of the Republic is elected by direct popular vote for a six-year term, renewable once, and can only be deposed by popular referendum supported by a majority in both houses. He appoints a Federal Chancellor, normally the leader of the strongest political party, who then proposes candidates for ministerial appointments. Separate ministers are nominated for foreign affairs; economic affairs; labour and social affairs; finance; federal affairs and administrative reform; women's affairs; health, sports and consumer protection; the interior; justice; defence; agriculture and forestry; the environment, youth and family affairs; education and the arts; the public economy and transport; and science and research.

An important though less visible aspect of Austrian society is the principle of *Sozialpartnerschaft*. Born of the frustrations and inadequacies of the First Republic, this consensus approach to running a country has served the Second Republic well.

The lessons learned in the inter-war period, economic, political and social, predisposed all players in the game to cooperate closely. Under the 'social partnership' the three principal estates - business and industry, organised labour and the farming community (in 1945 still a major component of the Austrian economy) - are permanently represented at government level through their respective federal chambers. Ministries work closely with them on detailed implementation of legislation and day-to-day management of the economy.

The sense of the common good engendered by this system is such that, by the standards of their equivalents in other countries, these chambers are at times seen to be putting the national interest ahead of that of their members or of individual pressure groups. All parties contribute to careful control of wages and prices. In the run-up to the referendum the agricultural chamber was a major factor in persuading the farmers to switch from fierce opposition to qualified support for accession to the European Union.

Wages and prices are the responsibility of a *Paritätische Kommission* (parity commission), a system that will be found in some other countries of the EU. An informal assembly, it comprises delegates from the federal trade union, the ÖGB; the chamber (as opposed to union) representing organised labour; the business and industry chamber; the agricultural chamber; the National Bank; and representatives of various ministries (economic affairs, labour and social affairs, and agriculture and forestry). Since all decisions have to be unanimous, there is a strong incentive to compromise. Moreover, the commission itself has no powers: it is up to the representative bodies to win acceptance of these decisions by their members. Throughout the leitmotiv is compromise and consensus.

This is inevitably a cumbersome way of running a country. In the words of a special report by the *International Herald Tribune* published end-1994, "critics say the partnership system is overly politicized, stifles entrepreneurship, and is too cozy an arrangement to survive in a world of increasing cross-border competition." Alexander Maculan, who heads up a major Austrian construction company, calls the chamber system "a relic of the past." He speaks for a growing group of critics who, while acknowledging efforts to achieve greater transparency in government, still feel the system is too complicated and fear the influence of the big lobbies.

But the system's defenders will point to the low unemployment rate as evidence of the success of the social partnership system, regardless of which unemployment figures you take. In early-1994, the OECD estimate was 4.6 per cent. Moreover, in recent years, the time lost through the rare strikes in Austrian industry has averaged six seconds per worker per year.

Whatever the pro's and con's of Austria's social partnership philosophy, it will inevitably have to yield to standards of governance imposed by accession to the European Union. Moreover many of the younger generation of Austrians reject the idea of having the country run in secret conclave by an inner circle of nominees.

Hopefully, membership of the Union will be seen as a step in the right direction, although there is fear of an anonymous inner circle of Eurocrats in Brussels.

Advancing education

The Austrian educational system, essentially a product of the 19th century, nonetheless served the country well in the early post-war years. Since the end of the 1960s, however, it has been going through a gradual transformation to meet the demands of a fast-changing world.

All holders of the *Matura*, the upper secondary school leaving certificate which is the equivalent of the German *Abitur* and the French *Baccalaureat*, qualify for university admission. Four years' successful completion of a university curriculum leads to the title of *Magister*, at least two intensive years more to a *Doktorat*.

Austria currently has twelve universities: three traditional ones (Vienna comprising five separate institutions, Graz and Innsbruck), three of fairly recent creation (Salzburg, Linz and Klagenfurt), and six specialised institutions (engineering, economics, agriculture and forestry, veterinary medicine and the famous Leoben Mining University). There are currently some 150,000 students enrolled at Austrian universities and colleges, three times as many as 20 years ago.

University lecturers still tend to use the traditional *ex cathedra* approach to teaching common to countries like France and Italy. However the underlying trend - initiated in the 1920s, abandoned in the *Hitlerzeit* and resuscitated in the 1960s - is towards a more enlightened teaching system. The government also plans to reduce the time currently needed to complete a university education while, on the other hand, developing a comprehensive system for continuing education.

The record of Austria's universities in pioneering research efforts, pure or applied, has compared poorly with that of most EU countries. The Research Organisation Act of 1981 heralded a more structured initiative aimed at improving the contribution of universities to technological knowhow and at enhancing collaboration between academia and industry.

The latest broad development is the creation of a network of technical high schools (FHS) to bring Austria into line with the higher educational structure of other European Union countries, where universities providing theoretical education and technical colleges offering practical studies operate in parallel. Similar to Germany's *Fachhochschule*, these schools will also provide facilities integrating with the country's extremely successful 'dual training' or industry apprenticeship scheme. Altogether, nearly 140,000 young people between the ages of 19 and 25 are currently engaged in this scheme.

Austria's Ministry of Education and Culture has also invested considerable efforts and funds in initiatives aimed at strengthening the country's links with the new democracies on its eastern borders. Its *Kulturkontakt* programme trains German-language teachers for service in these countries. Austria, specifically Graz, is also the home of the European Centre for Foreign Languages (now operating under the aegis of the Council of Europe) which provides a forum for minority linguistic groups.

Advancing the infrastructure

Austria's transportation infrastructure reflects the dictates of the terrain even if the construction, as early as 1854, of the Semmering pass standard-gauge railway link demonstrated the country's ability to meet such challenges.

Today's transport policy continues to be influenced by the country's geography and the absence of major agglomerations outside Vienna and the larger provincial capitals. Two other factors play an increasing role: first Austria's strategic location between western and eastern Europe and, secondly, concern about the environment.

The latter was a hot issue in the accession negotiations with the EU, fuelled by fears of growing road transit traffic - partly as a result of Switzerland's intransigence in forcing all its transit traffic onto rail. Concerned by the fact that only one-quarter of traffic crosses Austria by train (compared with three-quarters of transit traffic in Switzerland), the government is examining various measures to encourage the transfer of goods traffic from road to rail, including the introduction of multi-modal systems.

The Austrian federal railway network (ÖBB) is adopting the dual structure favoured by some other European countries including Sweden, with track and operations under separate management, but will remain state-owned. Geography precludes the development of a TGV-type high-speed rail network: instead Austria is developing the concept of a *Hochleistungsbahn*, a high-performance rail system handling fast commuter and freight traffic.

As a member of the Central European Transport Ministers Conference, Austria is working with its neighbours to establish a coordinated transport policy for the region. Until the dismantling of the Iron Curtain, more than 70 per cent of east-west traffic was by rail: the subsequent growth in road traffic is prompting the government to achieve greater 'transparency' in comparative costings and thereby improve the competitiveness of the rail system.

Since the post-WWI inception of the well-meaning but ill-fated First Republic, Austria has had an impressive record in housing its people. The state was a pioneer in the construction of high-density apartment blocks, building low-rental apartments or flats for over 200,000 families in traditionally Socialist-ruled Vienna alone. These were often of enlightened design, like the Karl-Marx-Hof, though not necessarily to the taste of today's tenants. Like the Swiss, Austrian town-dwellers tend to rent, although apartments can be bought.

The tendency in the provinces is to buy or build a house. In Tyrol, it is not uncommon for the eldest son inheriting a farm property to transfer 1,000 m2 lots to his brothers and sisters so that they can then build their own homes - often oversize with the intention of renting out rooms to foreign holidaymakers.

Enhancement of the country's transportation infrastructure and growing urbanisation do not conflict with Austrians' genuine commitment to preserving their unique environment. The country is currently investing nearly two per cent of GDP in environmental protection of one type or another - a higher figure than any other European country. In the early-1990s as much as two-thirds of this expenditure was coming from the private sector.

For foreigners, one less immediately visible aspect of the country's infrastructure is its public media facilities. The tentacles of the *Proporz* system even extended into public radio and TV until a public outcry in the late-1960s prompted the government to put the ORF on a footing similar to Britain's BBC. An act signed in 1974 then ruled illegal any attempt to exert influence on the corporation by either governmental or any other source.

Despite being a public corporation the ORF, unlike the present BBC, enjoys the luxury of income from both licences and advertising. It operates with a compact team of professionals - currently producing six programmes, two on TV and four on radio - and should be lean enough to meet the oncoming competition: private radio stations in 1995, with private TV stations likely to follow.

A complex culture

When comparing Austria with the two Nordic new-comers, even the most casual observer is aware of one thing: the difference in the psyche. While Austria is just as, if not more, committed to the principles of consensus and social partnership, the 'softness' of the Nordic mindset is absent.

Another very important difference is that, compared with the relatively homogeneous cultures of Finland and Sweden, Austria is not one but many different cultures: Vienna, the southern provinces, Tyrol, Vorarlberg, etc. Yet, outside these westernmost provinces, Austrian culture tends to take its lead from Vienna.

There is a tendency, it seems embedded in history, for foreigners to be nasty about the Austrians. Amongst other things, detractors say the Austrian psyche is macho. This simplistic attitude contains an element of truth. Austria must be one of the few countries in Europe to have seriously contemplated making a husband's participation in the housework legally enforceable! Moreover a seminal research study undertaken by Geert Hofstede in the '70s (see box, page 46) rated Austria the most 'masculine' of European cultures.

By contrast, a series of image studies conducted internationally by Vienna University in the latter half of the '80s and the early '90s showed that foreigners' perception of Austria diverges from the findings of Hofstede's research.

Asked to evaluate Austria against its two German-speaking neighbours, Switzerland and Germany, citizens of the European Union's member states were almost unanimous in giving the highest rating to this country and its people on a number of scores: 'famous for its culture', 'charming', 'old-fashioned', 'pleasant', 'friendly', 'romantic'.

All these are, of course, the old clichés that the Austrians - and particularly the Viennese - have cultivated so well, and sometimes unwittingly, and that foreigners hold to so dearly. Yet the same sample rated the Austrians much lower than their neighbours in terms of industriousness - a perception that has definitely not been borne out by the country's economic performance since the early-'80s.

As Polly Platt, a Paris-based American author and consultant who spent a number of years in Vienna, says: "The Austrians like to cultivate this idea that they are terribly laid back, yet in reality they are extremely hard-working. Don't underestimate them!"

Certainly the 'icons' of Austria's culture have contributed generously to the country's image: at the high-cult end of the scale, the traditional New Year's Concert, Mozart's Salzburg, the Vienna Boys' Choir, the Spanish Riding Academy and the Opera Ball. At the low-cult end, the *Kaffeehauskultur* (arguably high-cult), *Sachertorte, Mozartkugel* truffles, *Wiener Schnitzel* and, of course, *Ländler*.

Mozartkugel and onions

Polly Platt describes the Austrians as "a nation with a Germanic passion for rules and Latin ingenuity for getting around them... with German efficiency, Latin love of fun and macho Slav individualism all sheltered in the same breast."

Rebellious response to regulations is not just an Austrian speciality. They share it with their southern neighbours, the Italians, from whom they have also learned some useful tricks. The Belgians, even the French (*'le Système D'*), demonstrate the same skill.

It seems that society's efforts at regulation bring out the anarchistic streak in the individual, more markedly so in Latin and Slav cultures (when all is said and done, Austria is as much a Latino-Slav country as it is a Germanic one!). It seems that realism ultimately prevails. Jörg Mauthe tells the story of the bureaucrat who had two signs on his office door: the first said "Entry strictly forbidden to all!" and the second "Mind the step!".

Anyway, if something's not in the statute book, then it's tolerated - whatever it may be. A longstanding British resident of Vienna comments that Austrians "just love beating the system which, admittedly, often takes the form of piffling rules and regulations. Unfortunately this also seems to have the effect of depriving them of civil courage. They don't stand up for their rights."

Whatever 'mix' is used to describe the Austrian psyche, it is always a complex one. In 'The Book of Austria', Ernest Marboe describes Austria's *genius loci* as "Gothic imagination, Hellenic spirit, Celtic love of form, and Slav melancholy." Hans-Georg Behr, on the other hand, speaks in his book 'Die österreichische Provokation' of "Bavarian [Bajuvar] love of life, Slavic melancholy, Balkan business sense, Levantine cunning and Hungarian temperament."

Whichever interpretation you prefer - Platt's, Marboe's or Behr's - it is evident that the Austrians are, to put it mildly, a complex people. As the saying goes, "Vienna is where East thinks it's West - and *vice versa*!"

The Austrian philosopher Ludwig Wittgenstein said: "I think the good Austrian mentality is particularly hard to understand, it is in a particular sense subtler than any other, and its reality is never on the side of probability!" Which is, for most people, probably one of the least unintelligible things Wittgenstein ever said.

Some would-be wit suggested that the Austrian mind was like a *Mozartkugel*, the chocolate-coated truffle, turned inside out with a soft exterior concealing a harder core*. It is true that the charm and courtesy of the Austrian character can resolve suddenly into a fierce opposition to anyone or anything that does not fall within convention. Viennese society can be implacable and unforgiving. Maybe that's why the libretto of Johann Strauss' *Die Fledermaus* features the memorable words, "happy is he who forgets what cannot be changed!" [*"Glücklich ist, wer vergißt, was doch nicht zu ändern ist!"*].

But a better, and more sympathetic, analogy is the one offered by a much-travelled Irish lady who said that understanding the Austrian, and especially the Viennese, psyche was like stripping the skins off an onion. You go on and on, and are never quite sure you've reached the core...

Austrians will readily agree with the dilemma that faces us foreigners. They know they are complex people, but have justifiably no reason to regret the fact. In any case, it is an historical imperative. No one could have lived through the history they have known - and absorbed so many different cultural influences - without becoming complex in the process. Their problem, if there is one now, is to adapt to the often more simplistic demands of the world of today and tomorrow.

---

* Things with soft centres seem to have a place in Austrian *Weltanschauung*. The author Gerhard Fritsch used *Punschkrapfen* [doughnuts with an alcohol filling] as symbols in his novel 'Katzenmusik'. And a government minister attacked Austrian lack of competitivity recently by citing the humble doughnut as an example of excessive division of labour - with bakers making the doughnuts and *Zückerbäcker* inserting the jam!

Masculinity v Femininity

A mammoth research study undertaken in the early-1970s by Professor Geert Hofstede, a Dutch social psychologist, identified a number of comparative 'dimensions' which help explain the value systems and behavioural characteristics of the different national cultures. One of these is what he calls the 'masculinity versus femininity dimension'.

In masculine societies, the social gender roles are distinct, with men reflecting such values as achievement, material success and power, and women espousing such values as tenderness and quality of life. In feminine societies, these latter values are to be found in members of both sexes.

Hofstede found that Austria came right at the top of the masculinity scale with a rating of 79, followed by Switzerland and Italy with 70, and Ireland with 68. By comparison the Nordic countries were grouped towards the bottom, 'feminine', end of the scale with Finland with 26, Norway with only 8 and Sweden with precisely 5!

These Nordic figures come as no surprise to readers who know those countries. But that Austria rates as the most 'masculine' of all the nations of western Europe? The progress made in applying the principles of consensus and social partnership suggest the country has come a long way since the early-'70s when Hofstede's study was done.

A people of paradoxes

In his book 'Der Kampf um der österreichische Identität', Friedrich Heer maintains that the Austrian psyche swings from high spirits to depression, from self-doubt to delusions of grandeur. This is echoed by the words of the late Professor

Erwin Ringel who, in his masterpiece 'Die österreichische Seele', said that the Austrians "oscillate between sentimental self-deprecation and boundless feelings of grandiosity." The fact that they so readily accepted his judgment and, for the most part, genuinely admired him for his insight and candidness, suggests that the second characteristic may be losing some of its force.

But self-deprecation is certainly still very much - too much - in evidence, particularly among the Viennese. It is the expression of a lack of self-assurance inherited from the trauma of the past century, with Austria relegated from the ranks of a world power to a small state with a large identity problem. Significantly the Austrian expatriate returned from the United States, to whom we referred earlier, remarks that "the Austrians are very sensitive to people who are not sure of themselves. This is because they are not sure of themselves either..."

Educated Austrians readily acknowledge this lack of self-assurance and will even insist that it goes much further back than the collapse of the old Empire.

In his book 'Die österreichische Provokation' Georg-Hans Behr asserts that his fellow-countrymen have a reluctance to commit themselves in words. This, he suggests, may help explain how the country came to turn out so many fine musicians...

Novelist Marianne Gruber maintains that lack of self-assurance is reflected in the fatalism typical of the Viennese mind and personified, more than three centuries ago, in the shadowy historical figure of Augustin, the folk-singer who fell into a burial pit during the great plague of 1679: *"O du lieber Augustin, alles ist jetzt hin!"* ["Oh, dear Augustin, it's all up with you!"].

Another old song asserts *"Der Tod, der muß ein Wiener sein"* ["Death must be a Viennese"]. And similarly morbid sentiments have a nasty habit of popping up even in the drinking songs of the *Heuriger*, those traditional establishments where the Viennese let their hair down.

The death cult is indeed part of the Austrian way of life, the ultimate aim being to ensure that everyone goes out in style. Even young people are known to adopt savings plans to ensure they get a fine funeral at the end of the road.

This bitter-sweet attitude to life prompts many people to talk or write in paradoxes. Herbert Eisenreich even used a paradox to sum up the Viennese perspective: *"Der Zweifel ist die Hoffnung"* ["Where there is doubt, there is hope"], inferring that you couldn't expect better than that! Doubt is expressed in the everyday comment: *"Wer weiß, ob es wahr ist?"* ["Who knows if it's true?"].

Erwin Ringel says that Siegmund Freud would have had to be deaf and blind not to stumble across the Austrians' complexes (again, the operative word is 'complex' with these intriguing people). He believes they develop in childhood through the authoritarian attitudes of parents who impose excessive standards of obedience, politeness and thrift: a love-hate relationship develops between the generations.

This is, once again, more complex than the *Kinderfeindlichkeit* [hostility towards children] that used to characterise German society. Moreover, many foreign residents find that the relationships between Austrian generations are fast changing for the better.

But attitudes die hard. Even the fact that Austrians now spend more money on their children than other Europeans may highlight the problem rather than belie it. Speaking of the Austrian husband with whom she was raising a family at the time, American Polly Platt says that "I was often furious at what I considered his medieval formulas for bringing up young children, some of them right out of the torture chamber." She was equally alarmed at the behaviour of the Austrian nurse who wound up the new-born so tightly in swaddling clothes that it was absolutely helpless.

Yet today, 25 years later, Polly Platt concedes that this and some of the other traditions - for instance, not letting a baby lie on its stomach - were not only better than her own, but have since been endorsed by the medical profession.

Erwin Ringel concludes that these childhood experiences create a dichotomy in the Austrian mind, with emotions oscillating between outward courtesy and conformity, on the one hand, and hidden resentment and jealousy on the other. He quotes the words of the Dutch composer Bernard van Beurden who, without being a sociologist, had the opportunity to study the Austrian psyche at close hand: "The Austrian has a two-roomed house. One room is bright and friendly, a well-furnished room where he receives his guests. The other room is dark, with the blinds down, locked, inaccessible, completely out-of-bounds to strangers."

Professor Ringel also cites research from the early-1980s which claims to show that "1.4 million Austrians (i.e. nearly 20 per cent of the population) have practically no contact with their friends, outside their place of work, in an average month" and that "married couples speak to one another an average of seven minutes per day [!]".

The idea that there is a disquieting element in the Austrian psyche is fuelled by vague talk about high suicide rates (the Austrians can't match their neighbours, the Hungarians, on this point), by a level of illegitimate births that had already reached alarming proportions in the 1930s, and by the fact that one in ten Austrian males owns a firearm.

A touch of other-worldness or, put more bluntly, suppressed wildness, is also evoked in references to Austrian womenfolk. Speaking of the ladies of Viennese society in his book 'The Austrians: Strange Tales from the Vienna Woods', Richard Bassett positively raves that "the hint of cruelty which plays about Eastern eyes, evoking the violence of the Mongol hordes combined with the softness of a Cimabue portrait, is particularly appealing." He then praises their sisters of more modest standing for their "unspoiled femininity, uninhibited sensual nature and uncritical attitude towards men." They sound far less complex...

Endorsement of this reality may come from the fact that Austrian men appreciate women and flirt with them more than most other Europeans, including the Italians.

A much travelled member of Viennese society, on hearing a foreigner comment that Austrians - or more accurately the Viennese - are 'sentimental schizos', retorted "you're absolutely right." But then, by virtue of his status, he could afford to say so.

Protocol and provinciality

As the ultimate expression of all that is Austrian, Viennese society inevitably exaggerates the country's foibles. It is not that long ago in history that you would hear the phrases *'Erste Gesellschaft'* and *'Zweite Gesellschaft'* to describe the upper orders, the former being the princes and counts, the latter the more recently created barons, the *haute bourgeoisie* and officialdom, whose numbers and titles were (and still are) a hangover from the old Empire.

Today this establishment has extended to include the banking and business elite and is sardonically dubbed the 'Döblinger Regiment', from the name of the suburb where many of these people live. The change is reflected in the comment of a socially alert observer who said *"Ich war gestern bei xyz und es war alles da, was Rang und keine Namen hat!"* ["I was at so-and-so's yesterday and all the people there had titles but no distinction!"].

There is little or no communication between these classes and the lower orders. The rigidity of the social infrastructure is still reflected in the stuffy conventionality and smug conformity of the bourgeois Viennese mentality, at least that part that represents the public persona. Mercifully, the younger generations show signs of developing minds of their own.

Like most of their compatriots, the Viennese are charming and courteous people with a gift for making the stranger feel wanted. What's more this interest is genuine. Contrary to what many foreigners might expect, they are more likely to put human values before social judgments. An expatriate comments that the Catholic tradition has taught the Austrians the art of being considerate towards their fellow beings, despite occasional and flagrant lapses.

Polly Platt found that, as a divorced woman living in a Catholic country, she was treated with sympathy, decency and respect: "They were loyal, supportive and had a great sense of fun. Some of their values could be classed as 'old-fashioned', but these have a very positive side."

These sentiments were echoed by the elderly expatriate lady referred to earlier: "Older people tend to be suspicious of informal contact but, when they know you are new to the country, they respond. And they will never fail to help you if they know you have a problem."

But the Austrians can be very negative. An English businesswoman married to an Austrian who has lived in Vienna for over 20 years says the standard retort to almost any professional request is *"Unmöglich, das kann man nicht"* ["Impossible, it can't be done"]. "They're not easy to get to know but, once you know them, they're delightful people", she concludes, "but they're so negative."

Variations on this theme noted by British journalist Nicholas Parsons include *"Das hamma noch nie gemacht"* ["We've never done that"], *"Das hamma immer schon so gemacht"* ["We've always done it that way"] and *"Da könnt' ein jeder kommen"* ["Then anyone could come along"].

Another variant, extending to life generally, runs *"Kann man eh nichts machen!"* ["Nothing to be done about it!].

Bill Bryson notes, beneath the exterior charm, the occasional irritability of Viennese tradespeople. Yet even he, as an 'investigative journalist', found no evidence to support the notion, still alive in many people's heads, that the Viennese are the most disagreeable people in Europe. Again, attitudes die hard!

The stranger inevitably judges to his or her own standards. He or she finds the courtesy, the formalities, a little too overbearing for his or her tastes. That reflects as much on the stranger as on the Viennese. *Autre pays, autres moeurs*, that's all.

By comparison, the behaviour of ordinary people from the provinces can be starkly different from that of the Viennese - simple and direct. The most strikingly different are the Vorarlbergers, who avoid ostentation and are reserved in speech and gesture. You might say that they are 'typically Swabian' since they are descended from the Alemanni tribes who moved there from the Valais region of Switzerland. They even ape the work ethic and the vocabulary of the Swabians with their *"schaffa, schaffa, husle baua"* ["work, work, build your own house"].

Other elements of Austrian provincial society, particularly the townsfolk, ape Viennese mannerisms - grandiose gestures and utterances like *"Habe die Ehre, Herr Generaldirektor"* and *"Küß die Hand, gnädige Frau"* - only to look, to the untutored foreigner, unbelievably comic.

If you've a taste for this kind of thing, no problem. If you don't, you'll find it heavy going. But remember that the provincial societies of other European countries demonstrate the same traits.

Style and symbolism

Vienna is a sensationally attractive and superbly run city that puts many other capitals to shame (the Austrian who said, not long ago, that "Vienna remains Vienna, and that's the worst one can say of this city" was appropriately ambiguous). Its people, particularly the young, have an inborn sense of style that must owe something to the Austro-Hungarian imperial tradition: they radiate self-awareness without pretentiousness*. Sometimes, of course, the urge to show a touch of class gets out of hand. Austria, like Britain, is starting to make excessive use of a particularly mindless form of symbolism: a personalised car numberplate.

According to Robert Menasse symbolism is an important component of public life: "In Austria it's not the case that something said or done in public is either right or wrong, it either has symbolic value or it doesn't. It's not a question of whether it's effective or ineffective, it either has symbolic power or not."

There has been a tradition for public life in general, and politics in particular, to be conducted in a paternalistic manner, with the appropriate admixture of condescension and largesse. Even the concept of the 'social partnership' was an act of paternalism by the parties of the time. The parties existed before the country did!

In the words of a senior TV journalist, "the development of civil society in our country has always been inhibited by the tendency of the *Obrigkeit*, the government and its senior administrators, to do everything 'from the top down'. Bruno Kreisky was the first to break the mould: he was the first

---

* The Viennese tell a charming story about Otto von Habsburg asking his valet to turn on the television set. A football match is in progress. "What's the match?", asks Otto. "Austria-Hungary", replies the valet. "Ah", says Otto, "but who are they playing against?"

cosmopolitan politician we had, not a *Dorfpolitiker* [village politician]." Today any citizen with a grievance against bureaucracy can appeal through the institution of the *Volksanwalt* [People's Lawyer].

One aspect of their past that Austrians evidently have difficulty breaking with - and that they share with other nationalities, in particular the Germans and the French - is a taste for professional titles. The proverbial *Herr Doktor Doktor* really exists. There is in addition a host of *Rats* (various levels of public official), two varieties of *OberAmts-Rat*, *ordentliche* and *unordentliche*, as well as *Hofrat*, *Ministerialrat*, *Magistratsrat*, even *Oberbaurat* and *Kommerzialrat*.

All of this is a very belated hangover from the days of the Austro-Hungarian Empire when public officialdom came next to godliness and even attracted artistic souls like the poet Franz Grillparzer as a way of earning a living. Many of these officials were Czechs working for the Bohemian-Austrian Hofkanzlei and were instructed by Maria-Theresia to learn German, which they did.

In his book 'Die österreichische Provokation' Hans-Georg Behr suggests that the average Austrian has two ambitions in life: first to be a public official, secondly to have a fine funeral - something that is guaranteed if he or she reaches the rank of senior civil servant. Behr then talks about "pompous titles, of which the most honoured in the Republic, and the most prized even by anti-monarchist socialists, is that of Hofrat..."

In the same spirit, every university graduate parades the term *Magister* in front of his name. At worst, and with advancing age, he or she will be addressed as *"Herr Professor"*, a distinction that is automatically accorded to every secondary school teacher and, in one instance, was inadvertently attributed to a railway signalman.

This genuflecting reflex is so deeply ingrained that it extends into intimate relationships, leading to kafkaesque exchanges like *"Wie geht's Dir, Herr Magistratsrat?"*, *"Gut! Und Dir, Herr Kommerzialrat?"*

No one can dispute Vienna's status as a cultural centre. The density of bookshops in the city's 'First District' must exceed that of any other city in Europe - even if, according to some people in the trade, the Viennese buy books to give to their friends (or enemies) and not to read themselves.

Yet the Viennese support the performing arts in the same way that other Europeans support their local football club: they also tend to riot the same way if they don't approve of the performance. And for many Viennese a season ticket to the Burgtheater or the opera is the best evidence possible of their social status.

Another important aspect of Vienna's cultural life is of course the *Kaffeehauskultur* - a uniquely central European phenomenon which subsists throughout the old territories of the Austro-Hungarian Empire. "The Viennese always have time for a coffee", comments a city administrator. "The *Kaffeehaus* plays a vital part in the life of the city - people use it to entertain, to talk business, just to read and relax" (with the help of a rich choice of newspapers and, in some cases, a bookcase full of dictionaries!). It is a home away from home.

By any standard, Vienna is a spectacularly beautiful city. Whereas some of its historic buildings, particularly the heavy baroque structures that ornament the Ringstraße, may be a bit overblown for foreign tastes, the city's contemporary architecture - witness the government offices on the Radetskystraße or the Haus Haas next to the Stephansdom - is nothing short of breathtaking.

"A Martian coming to earth would unhesitatingly land at Vienna, thinking it the capital of the planet", says Bill Bryson, who rates the Kärtnerstraße and Graben as "the finest pedestrian thoroughfare in Europe." Vienna's public transport system and the city's administration generally are as good as, if not better than, any to be found in Europe. Even as hostile a resident as *The Spectator*'s Edward Lucas concedes that "the streets are safe at almost any hour of the day or night. Public transport is superb." Yet still 70 per cent of commuters, of whom there are 180,000, come into Vienna by car.

Much the same can be said about Austria's other cities: they are neat, well-run and hospitable. Speaking of Innsbruck, Bill Bryson says "it is carefully preserved without having the managed feel of an open-air museum." Nigel Andrews of the *Financial Times,* writing about the provincial capital of Styria, says "grandeur in Graz jostles with an endearing laid-backness." The country has no slums to speak of. There are lots of well-off, even reasonably wealthy, people. Yet the rich, by European Union standards, can be counted on the fingers of two pairs of hands.

This, maybe more than anything else, testifies to the success of the country's distinctive approach to democracy since WWII. It inevitably implied a degree of conformism, even fatalism, on the part of ordinary people. Yet the system worked and has raised the country to the ranks of the ten richest nations in the world. Having achieved material prosperity, maybe the Austrians can reinstate themselves as one of the main contributors to European culture.

Foreigners are astonished at the way Austrians, particularly intellectuals, still agonise over the identity and vocation of the country. Surely it is time to lay these ghosts to rest.

As people unduly sensitive to the idea of seeming 'provincial' to the rest of the world, the Austrians are entitled to view accession to the European Union as the opportunity to be more cosmopolitan once again, while at the same time adjusting their policies to the realities of the new Europe. Shades of glories past...

The industrious Austrians

The World Competitiveness Report - published jointly by IMD, the International Institute for Management Development, and the World Economic Forum - is a respected annual review of the performance of nations. The 1994 edition of this study polled the opinions of 16,500 senior business executives, including samples from each of the European countries.

Although it had fallen two places since the previous year's study, Austria came ninth out of 44 countries in the world competitiveness stakes, after Singapore, New Zealand, Hong Kong, Denmark, Switzerland, Sweden, the Netherlands and Germany. On workforce skills and attitudes, the country ranked seventh overall.

Austrian industry is an effective if little-known performer in European and international markets. It is little-known because it has no multinationals in the accepted sense and few well-known brands. Most of its industries are SMEs operating in niche markets and some, if not many, of these markets are in eastern rather then western Europe. Yet these niche markets are often significant technologically and Austria's market leaders frequently dominate in these technologies.

Foreigners' perception of Austrian industry is clouded by memories of old and temporarily faded glories - in particular the state-owned VOEST steelmaking and engineering combine and the Steyr automotive group - as well as by ignorance of contemporary realities. As a side-effect of the concept of social partnership, these industries were too readily bank-rolled by government and, as happened in the case of VOEST, bailed out. In fact VOEST (VOEST-Alpine as it is known today) is in the process of being privatised and Steyr is performing effectively in new fields of endeavour like 4x4-wheel drive technology.

Part of the explanation also lies in Austria's past dependence on Czech industry, both before and after the collapse of the Austro-Hungarian Empire. It was the Czech lands that contributed 70 per cent of the Empire's industrial output at the end of the last century and, even in 1937, Czech GDP was far higher than Austria's.

The only major players in the economy of the First Republic were a few large corporations active in the traditional areas of iron and steel, engineering, oil and chemicals, plus of course forestry, agriculture and tourism. The impressive growth of the mainly family-owned *Mittelstand* sector - often large companies by European SME standards - is a reflection of the stable economic policies pursued by the government in post-WWII years. Moreover, recent experience has shown that this sector is particularly resistant to recession, a factor which helps explain the country's strikingly low unemployment rate.

Today iron and steel is still a vibrant element of the Austrian economy characterised by two companies now in the process of being privatised, VOEST-Alpine and Böhler Uddeholm. The first of these, famous for its highly successful LD steelmaking technology, is now commercialising the promising COREX direct reduction process through its VOEST-Alpine Anlagenbau subsidiary. Böhler Uddeholm is proving equally successful on international markets with its highly refined speciality steels. A star performer in the private sector is Metallwerk Plansee, a world leader in powder metallurgy.

The country's achievements in metallurgy owe much to the healthy influence of the materials sciences faculty of the Leoben Mining University in Styria, which provides students with a high level of skills and collaborates actively with the private sector on both basic and applied research.

The chemical and petrochemical sectors are also competitive internationally, having submitted to the rationalisation processes common to the industry. Austria has important though often relatively low-value reserves of minerals, notably magnesium (Radenthein), wolfram, salt, lead/zinc and clays. A major resource is hydro-electric power, both on the Danube and in the mountainous western provinces of the country.

Engineering in all its forms, extending to measuring instrumentation and medical equipment, is where the SME sector is most in evidence, with specialist companies like AVL (diesel engines), Engel (plastics machinery), Plasser & Theurer who make those little yellow tracklaying machines that everyone thinks are Swiss, and Doppelmayr who combined technical and marketing skills to grab the world ski-lift market back from the Americans. The last of these is a representative of a particularly vigorous SME economy in the westernmost province of Vorarlberg: the province has a per capita export performance six times higher than that of the US and three times higher than Japan.

Steyr, with its 4x4-wheel drive technology, and other industries in the Graz area have carved a reputation as competitive subcontractors and suppliers to both the German and the Japanese automobile industries (partly by offering preferential import duty treatment on completed cars in the case of the latter). And, despite the fact that they have only a small vehicle manufacturing industry, the Austrians manage to return a favourable net balance of trade on automobile-related products.

Further development of the Austrian *Mittelstand* sector depends largely on capitalisation and financing. Few SMEs are quoted on the Vienna stock exchange, although changes in 1980 in the laws governing Austria's capital markets have resulted in some initiatives since the end-'80s, including the successful Mayr-Meinhof issue in 1994.

Though they are Europe's great savers, the Austrians prefer to put their economies into low-interest accounts. Little of this money finds its way into industry, while venture capital potential is blunted by the fact that the beneficiary has to accept a nominee on the board. The big banks - some of which, still to be privatised, act as foster-parents to the nationalised industries - have some way to go in offering facilities that will appeal to the SME sector.

In the opinion of the German magazine *Wirtschaftswoche*, the Austrian worker is industrious, intelligent and takes a pride in his work. At the time of writing, productivity is on a par with German productivity, yet wage rates are 20 per cent lower. Manufacturers like BMW, who use engines produced in Styria, and Chrysler, who manufacture their Voyager minivan in Graz, are impressed by the low claim and defect rates. In the words of the *Financial Times*, "strikes are practically unknown." The American chief executive of a metalworking multinational reports that his Austrian plant is so cost-effective that "there is no point in even looking at the possibility of transferring production to eastern Europe."

Evidently Austria's bosses are aware of their country's potential. Questioned in the World Competitiveness Report, they emphasized the importance of their society's values - hard work, loyalty, etc - in supporting competitiveness.

Austria's present government is heir to an excessive level of nationalisation. This was incurred partly through adherence to the Republic's principles of social partnership, partly through the need to nationalise some previously German-controlled heavy industries to avoid them being dismantled under the reparations programme. But, even before entry to the European Union, the administration had committed itself to a progressive and wide-reaching programme of privatisation under the aegis of the ÖIAG state holding company.

Ten years ago, 20 per cent of the economy was state-owned, today the figure is 10 per cent. Two out of every 10 people in the Austrian workforce are employed by the state. By 1997 all major nationalised industries, with the notable exception of mining and the railways, will have been privatised to the extent of at least 51 per cent of their share capital.

Membership of the European Union has also enhanced Austria's attraction as a strategically placed manufacturing location: there has been a big surge in foreign investment since the results of the referendum became known. The ICD, Austria's inward investment agency, claims that foreign businesses are particularly attracted by the country's "state-of-the-art infrastructure and bottom-line profitability."

Agriculture and tourism

Manufacturing industry, including the production of artisanal goods, represents 32 per cent of Austria's total GNP. Fifteen per cent comes from tourism and less than 3 percent from agriculture, the balance being made up essentially by services.

Austria applies a balanced strategy to the development of tourism, with the promotional budget evenly spread between summer and winter tourism. The country has recently seen a fall-off in the number of winter holidaymakers from its main market, Germany, more as a consequence of past over-indulgence in such activities by Germans than as a result of the recession.

Half a million Austrians are active full-time or part-time in the tourist industry. The many private ventures, including initiatives by farmers looking for a supplementary income, have left the industry heavily indebted and sensitive to swings in the economy. But the industry benefits from the compulsory learning of English in secondary schools and from the reputation of its hotel schools and other vocational institutions.

Despite its relative unimportance as a contributor to GNP, Austrian agriculture is still an important element in the country's life. Moreover it benefits from a symbiotic relationship with tourism.

Both industries have to face up to the realities of major regional variations in geography and climate. While the Alps at the western end of the country offer oxygen-laden summers and crisp cold winters, with some valley floors seeing no sun for nearly two months of the year, the easternmost province of Burgenland offers hints of the Hungarian puszta. While the hilly Waldviertel region north of the Danube bears the brunt of harsh northerly winds, the sheltered provinces of the south enjoy long hot summers with, conveniently, a thunderstorm most evenings to release excess humidity.

Even before negotiations on access to the Union, Austria's farmers had been struggling manfully to adjust to changing market conditions. The average size of the country's 260,000 agricultural enterprises is 28 hectares (± 70 acres), of which only half is on average exploitable for farming purposes. Even this modest figure is skewed by the existence of some very large agricultural estates owned by nobility or the monastic orders, mainly in Lower Austria and Burgenland.

The precarious existence of much of Austria's agricultural community is demonstrated by the high proportion of part-time farmers (60 per cent overall and as high as 95 per cent in the Landeck area of Tyrol) and by the fact that over five per cent have abandoned the industry in the last few years. 55 per cent of those still engaged in farming are over 55 years old.

Stagnation in income and growing international competition did nothing to help win support from the agricultural community for accession to the European Union. In 1987, 80-

90 per cent of farmers were against membership. It was only gentle persuasion by the federal agricultural chambers and patient negotiation of certain key financial concessions with the Union by government that prevented a massive farmers' vote against entry.

The government has practised a policy of selective subsidies to small farmers to protect marginal economies and maintain local cultures and lifestyles, a programme adopted in 1987 under the title *Ökosoziale Agrarpolitik*. Turning abandoned agricultural land over to forestry is not necessarily the solution since, apart from the fact that Austria already has 800,000 hectares (±3,000 square miles) of state-owned forest, neither local communities nor their holidaymaking customers, skiers in particular, are anxious to see exclusively tree-covered landscapes. The threat of Waldsterben is under control and timber stands, constantly replenished, are already more than enough to meet the demands of the country's wood, pulp and paper industries.

Another concern is the 'second residence' phenomenon, which had already been a major issue in Denmark. Predominantly elderly Germans have been acquiring property with a view to retirement. The government now demands proof from the purchaser, Austrian or foreign, that the land will still continue to be exploited for agricultural purposes. Many farmers are in fact selling parcels of land to family and friends, who then build homes for themselves with separate apartments for rental to holidaymakers.

Austria's farmers and food processers are jealous of their reputation for quality which, by association, took a hard knock at the time of the 1985 wine scandal. Government quality control of all foodstuffs and beverages is strict and, in many cases, exceeds EU standards.

Increasingly, farmers and producers are combining in *Qualitätsgemeinschaften* to ensure uniformly good products and improve their international marketing. They need to do this since present standards and volumes make it difficult to compete with big producers from Germany and elsewhere. They need to act quickly since, in the months since accession to the European Union, foreign imports have swamped the Austrian market for dairy products. Consumers are delighted with the increased variety and lower prices, manufacturers and farmers far less so.

The Austrian wine industry, which employs some 40,000 people, is now putting the emphasis on improved marketing of higher-value-added quality wines, particularly those from the Wachau region on the Danube.

Austrians are very attached to their gastronomic traditions, as evidenced by the fuss over EU rules on the denomination of products. *Kartoffelsalat* [potato salad] is OK for the Germans but in Austria, to take the words of a poster campaign just prior to accession, *Erdäpfelsalat bleibt Erdäpfelsalat!*

Consensus, not confrontation

Austrian business used to be epitomised by the image of the little man with the inevitable hat and a plastic briefcase, often containing his lunch and little else.

That image is long out of date though, with the predominance of the *Mittelstand* in industry, the Austrian executive may still seem modestly folkloric to the multinational community. It is for example still the case that the average businessman aged 40 or over will be a poor speaker of foreign languages including English, now a compulsory subject at school.

Marketing skills and even basic business sense also need to be developed. In the words of Maria Schaumayer, president of the Austrian National Bank, "our small and medium sized companies are not accustomed to being in a buyers' market. It will take them a while to learn to bargain." Business skills are now an educational priority. The Federal Chamber of Commerce operates a highly regarded management school at Hernstein in Lower Austria. Other institutions offering management training include the Management Center Vorarlberg, and the MDI and the Business Circle in Vienna.

Most, though not all, foreign business people will confirm that working with Austrians is by and large a pleasant experience. The Viennese, who often demonstrate an "almost Latin politeness", in the words of one of them, are agreeable and relaxed negotiators. A senior trade official goes to the heart of the matter when he says that "people prefer the Austrians because we're more open and easy-going than the Germans, more prepared to compromise."

A foreign businessman puts it more trenchantly: "Austrians... do not have set rules. They see which way the wind is blowing and act accordingly." Another, the CEO of an American multinational, speaks enthusiastically of the younger generation of Austrian manager: "They're good business people, extremely conscientious and hardworking, yet low-key. But", he adds, "you sometimes get the feeling that they're 'working around the edge'."

Commitment to the Union will not prevent Austria from seeking closer integration with its neighbours in central and eastern Europe. Since 1989 the country has been associated, along with Italy, in the *Pentagonale* initiative involving Hungary, the Czech Republic and the old Yugoslavia (now known as the *Initiative Mitteleuropa*, with the inclusion of Poland). A project has been set up to harmonise transportation policies and other aspects of economic life.

The country's success in developing exports to and business relationships with its neighbours to the east may help explain the relatively modest impact of the recession on Austria. Currently exports to neighbouring central and eastern European markets represent nearly 15 per cent of total

Long on consensus, short on strategy

A number of surveys have been made of the Austrian business culture and management styles, notably those undertaken by Professor Andrew Kakabadse of the UK's Cranfield School of Management. From one such study conducted among over 300 top managers in 1993, the Cranfield team concluded that Austrian managers practise "a non-confrontational style of operation... a desire to agree, achieve consensus, and avoid disharmony."

This view was elaborated in the comments of one of the participants in the study: "I think Austrian managers are goal- and objectives-oriented, like... German managers. But we identify a goal and look for the best possible way to reach this goal. German managers see a goal, see their present situation and see a line. I think Austrian managers are really able to act according to situations, and are sensitive to human beings without losing [sight of] the main objectives and reaching the goals."

The survey also revealed that Austrian managers have difficulty in dealing openly and effectively with long-term strategic and structural issues with their top management teams. "Because of the way in which they have traditionally been operating, Austrian managers appear to be comparatively inexperienced in dealing in the long term. As a result of this inexperience, discussion within top management teams becomes divisive and difficult." It may be precisely this short-term orientation that helped the Austrian *Mittelstand* respond so swiftly and effectively to changing market conditions in the opening years of the 90s!

A more recent Cranfield study, 'Boardroom Skills for Europe', examined the management styles of eight European countries including Austria. Identifying four basic styles - Inspirational (essentially British and Spanish),

Elitist (almost exclusively French), Consensual (Nordic) and Directive - the survey placed Austria in the last category next to the Germans. This conclusion to some extent challenges the view of the manager quoted earlier: the desire for consensus, which characterises every facet of life in the Second Republic, runs counter to the search for a functional focus, which is typical of the German business culture.

The study highlights the poor quality of in-company dialogue resulting from this Directive style. An Austrian participant in the survey, the chief executive of a well-known international corporation, commented that "relationships are very sensitive in Austrian and German companies. People talk to each other quite openly when talking to each other about jobs but, when it gets to more sensitive issues about people or company strategy, nobody dare say anything so nothing gets solved. It's really bad... we all know things could be better." This sounds suspiciously like the effect of what Geert Hofstede, the Dutch guru of organisational anthropology, calls 'Uncertainty Avoidance'.

exports, a situation that may change with Austria's accession to the European Union.

Inevitably Austrian entrepreneurs are nervous about the competition from their neighbours to the east, not only in terms of inroads into the Austrian market as product quality improves, but also as alternative manufacturing locations. In the words of an Austrian businessman interviewed by the *Financial Times*, "for the cost of running a small factory with 50 workers here, you can move to Bratislava and employ more than 200 workers."

Some Austrian manufacturers - the Wolford hosiery company in Vorarlberg is a good example - have reacted imaginatively by moving upmarket to avoid head-on competition from low-cost competitors. Others have decided that the best form of defence is attack. At the time of publication there were over 12,000 Austrian direct investments in eastern Europe.

Austria can easily justify its claims to being an ideal departure point for organisations attacking central and eastern European markets. In addition to its record of political stability and sound economic management since WWII, Vienna offers a highly educated executive/administrative workforce, many of them familiar with some of the languages spoken to the east. These factors have not escaped the attention of the multinationals, many of whom now have their coordination offices for eastern Europe in Vienna.

Speaking to an international journalist, Debbie Lloyd of the US software manufacturer Oracle, added the x-factor: "Vienna is in the West but it has an East European orientation - all the historical ties with the Habsburg Empire, Romania, Bohemia. Logistically it's practically ideal because of plane and train connections. But", she added with reason, "it's so expensive!"

But you can't have everything...

The
NewComers

Finland

Finland,
the last frontier

One not insignificant link between Austria and Finland is the almond pralines produced by a Finnish company, Fazer. They are judged superb even by people who claim not to like chocolate. They are called 'Wiener Nougat'.

In most other respects the two countries are worlds apart. Finland is a Lutheran country where Austria is severely Catholic. Finland is flattish where Austria is decidedly bumpy. Finns appear to be withdrawing where Austrians are forthcoming.

But these countries have two things in common. Both have a special relationship with the countries of eastern Europe. And both have been strongly influenced by German culture and German social and educational philosophy.

Both of these countries, which are joining the Union at a key juncture in the evolution of Europe, are building a new and distinctive identity from their historical foundations.

But of the three new member nations - Austria, Finland and Sweden - Finland is the one on the raw edge of Europe and the one the reader is least likely to have visited.

Geographically, Finland is the fifth largest country of the European Union, one-third of it above the Arctic Circle, and the one which leans furthest to the east. In fact, Helsinki is on the same longitude as Athens, one hour ahead of most other EU countries.

It is distant, very distant - and in that fact alone assumes the lineaments of the exotic by most European standards, not even recognisable in its own name: *Suomi*.

"What is my homeland?" wrote one of the country's best known poets, Edith Södergran, in a 1920s work called, appropriately enough, "The Shadow of the Future".

"What is my homeland? Is it far-off, star-strewn Finland?

No matter what it is. Low stones, roll on flat shores.

I stand on your grey granite as on a certainty."

Granite, certainly, shaved by the Ice Age into smooth undulations which are separated by some 200,000 lakes surrounding a mere 98,000 islands.

But those are only the inland islands. There are a further 81,000 in the Baltic, especially in the south-west between Finland and Sweden.

It is almost superfluous to add that this landmass, at once so solid yet fragmented, is mostly covered by forest below the Arctic Circle. In the absence of the spectacular (no fjords or alps) and only gentle hills, the defining characteristics of the Finnish landscape are water and the colossal forests of pine, birch and spruce.

In this limpid vastness exists a small population, more or less five million people, who make up 35 per cent of the world's population north of latitude 60°N.

Who are they? This is not a facetious question because, while self-evidently a Nordic people, they are ethnically different from their sister countries. Here we get into the realms of speculation and academic controversy. It is claimed that most of the earliest settlers, who arrived here around 7,000 BC, had done so after trekking over generations from some indeterminate location south of the Ural Mountains. Yet most of the immigrants turned up about 2,000 years ago and were first mentioned by others in 1470 AD. In the late-18th century, Finland was known as the "land of witches".

What is not supposition is that in their language, appearance and certain aspects of their culture the Finns, like the Estonians across the Gulf, are Fenno-Ugrians*.

In layman's terms, they are anything but Vikings. They look different from other Nordics, with higher cheekbones and squarer skulls, sometimes with slightly slanted eyes. Some of them have a characteristic which fascinates anthropologists, a fold of skin between eyebrow and eyelid not found elsewhere in Europe.

Just as one can tell the difference between, say, a Celt and an Anglo-Saxon, the distinctive looks of the Finns can soon be distinguished from the other Nordic nations, even though most of today's Finns are anthropologically 'western' in origin.

But this word 'western' can in no sense be applied to the Finnish language, which is said to be one of the world's most difficult - and for which no other fluency can prepare one because of its unique structure, complications and opacity. It is one of Europe's few non Indo-European languages.

It has no masculine or feminine, no prepositions, no definite or indefinite articles - and that's just to tease the tyro student! After that, it starts to get damned difficult: fifteen case endings, compound words as long as your forearm, stem words which virtually disappear, word forms so transformed they do not feature, as such, in dictionaries.

Even then you have merely laid out your *veitsi* [knife] and *haarukka* [fork] for the linguistics feast to come. So it is that, both at home or abroad, Finns speaking together can do so with the 99 per cent certainty they will not be under-

---

* Finno-Ugrian in anglicised form.

stood by anyone else. This could offer some professional and personal advantages in the EU context, of course.

Add the fact that Finland is one of the most homogeneous countries in Western Europe and it follows that the Finns have an extremely well developed sense of their identity and culture - and also of their "apartness". If something alien or unfamiliar is put to them, the retort to fend it off is "but I'm a Finn" as if that explains their reaction. And then one realises that, as a matter of fact, it does.

"They are a people that nobody in the world could possibly feel sorry for", Jan Morris wrote a decade ago in an essay about Helsinki. "They are as tough as nails, and twice as spiky."

Spiky? Ouch, yet that's for sure - and they're defensive-aggressive too. "Why are you wearing those socks?", a complete stranger demanded of an innocent foreigner in a Helsinki street, objecting to their bright blue.

If one criticises a national characteristic or a Finnish public figure, it's rather like being in the boots of that unfortunate policeman called in to intervene in a domestic dispute. Previous enmities are instantly buried in a united effort to do down the interloper. The Finns tear each other apart with a special venom and envy, but god help an outsider who might challenge some feature of, or personality in, Finnish society!

Suddenly the truth of that old saying is neon-bright: "Finland is not a country, it's a club." Or, it might be added, a tribe. So, if you are not a member, you absolutely have to play by the members' rules. For a tough people, they are surprisingly thin-skinned.

But praise and approval are also unwelcome, they make Finns uncomfortable and self-deprecating. A frequent visitor will be asked "Why do you keep coming back?", as though there was something wrong with him or her. And the same person will have to be on the alert for another direct question: "What do you think of the Finns?" This is not just conversation-making. The Finns really want to know, warts and all, though it may not be such a good idea to include the blemishes when replying.

Long before joining the European Union, some Finns were expressing anxiety about the future of Finnish culture and whether, indeed, it had a future. Part of a typical 'small country complex' - or were there, are there, other concerns?

Many of those Finns opposed to EU membership felt that the national identity would be swamped, while conveniently overlooking the existing brash and persuasive influence of American pop culture on the country. Alone among European nations, Finland has an indigenous form of baseball...

It is nonsense, we believe, to imagine Finnish culture being undermined by influences from 'Europe' - as Finns still refer to it, meaning, in effect, anything south of the Baltic. It could be argued that Finnish culture has much to gain from the stimulus and influences of others. Vice versa, come to that.

As with all Nordic countries, it was the relative isolation of Finland which served to reinforce the sense of self of a country which, before the days of mass tourism, had nothing to compare itself with.

Few foreigners visited Finland in the '50s and '60s. With its 1,300-kilometre contiguous frontier with what was then the Soviet Union, Finland was a sort of dead end. There was nowhere else to go from there.

To take a small but illuminating example, until the mid-'70s there were practically no foreign restaurants in Helsinki, still less in the provinces. The use of garlic in the kitchen was practically unknown, and even then generally took the form of garlic salt. It was potatoes and herring, potatoes and salmon and, if one tired of them, there was always salmon again or huge chunks of meat.

Today, relative to its size, Finland has as numerous a selection of foreign 'tables' as any other country - with a special fondness for Chinese cuisine plus reassuringly huge mounds of rice. And fondness for garlic is on the up and up...

Although there are still signs of a time-warp quaintness in Finland, recollecting a vivid world of over 30 years ago, these are now fewer - and they will doubtless decrease further as, in the cities especially, more cosmopolitan influences are brought to bear.

The drive to update or eliminate some of the more characteristically Finnish elements is masked everywhere - by for example giving shops, restaurants and so on inappropriate foreign names where previously they had perfectly fine, even romantic, Finnish ones.

Anyway, at a deeper level, any first-time visitor to Finland should remember the paradox of the antiquity of the land and the youthfulness of today's republic.

From Grand Duchy to 'Finnification'

For six hundred years, from 1200 AD, Finland was a part of the Kingdom of Sweden. During that period the Swedes and Russians engaged in three wars on Finnish territory. The last, in 1808, led to the occupation of Finland by Tsar Alexander I, to whom the Swedes ceded the country.

The Tsar made himself personally responsible for all Finnish matters. He turned Finland into an autonomous Grand Duchy of the Russian Empire and proved a benevolent overseer of the land - which is why his statue still commands Helsinki's main square in front of the Lutheran Cathedral.

The Tsar's motives were of course self-interested. A strong and peaceful Grand Duchy was the best forward defence for St Petersburg, his main preoccupation, and it would also help to trip the balance of Baltic power against Sweden.

For 108 years the status quo more or less remained. But in the late-1890s a separatist movement was already under way, the start of nationalism, of "Finnification".

This increasing self-assertion found its most dramatic expression in a general strike in 1905 which was the beginning of the end of the country's Grand Duchy status.

The Parliament was established the following year and, with it, a franchise system which included the women's vote, making Finland the first European nation to do so.

The separatists nonetheless had a protracted struggle on their hands because, despite the Tsar's enforced liberalisation of control, the Russians became increasingly aggressive to those civil servants and judges who were now defiant of Tsar-made laws and statutes.

We are indebted to Mikko Norros of *Finnfacts* for this A-Z of things Finnish:

A   Area (Finland): total 338,000 km2. Fifth largest country in Europe.

B   Banks: open for foreign exchange Mon-Fri from 09.15 to 16.15 hours.

C   Capital: Helsinki. Not 'Helsinky' or 'Hell sin sky'. Population 500,000, approximately.
Climate: in June the temperature varies from 18°C to 25°C. Normally not too much rain.

D   Distances: always long. Maximum distances 1,160 km from north to south and 540 km from east to west.

E   Exports: wood and paper 36%, metal products and machine industry 35.9%, chemicals 10.6%, basic metal industry 8.8%, textiles, clothing and leather 2.3%, other industries 6.4%.

F   Family: average size 2.7 persons.
Forests: forestry land accounts for 26 million hectares, ie 87% of the land area, and is mostly privately owned.

G   Government: republic. President, elected for 6-year term: Martti Ahtisaari. Parliament elected for four years. 200 MPs (79 women) from nine different parties.

H   History: a union with Sweden from the 12th century to 1809, when Finland became a Grand Duchy of Tsarist Russia. Independent since 6 December 1917.

I   Islands: total 179,584. We don't know who counted them. Europe's largest archipelago lies between Finland and Sweden.

J   Jewellery: famous brands include Lapponia and Kalevalakoru.

K   Keywords: sauna, Sibelius, *sisu* (endurance), *kippis* (cheers!) and *kiitos* (thankyou!). There are others, but we keep those to ourselves...

L   Language: impossible. Finnish is a Fenno- (Finno-) Ugrian tongue.
Lakes: we are still counting them.

M   Midnight Sun: the sun is constantly above the horizon in Lapland in June, July and August. In Helsinki it goes down for a couple of hours. Don't be worried if you wake up and think you've overslept. Look at your watch: it's probably 4 in the morning.

N   Nature: there are 2.2 million hectares of nature reserve. Take your compass.

O   Omnibuses: will take you just about anywhere.

P   Punctuality: a Finnish invention.

Q   Quiet people = Finns, except when they drink too much reindeer milk.

R   Religion: Lutheran 90%, Greek Orthodox 1%, other religions 1%, non-denominational 8%.

S   Sauna: see next chapter.

T   Time: GMT+2.

U   Universities: 19.

V   *Viili*: processed sour milk.

W   Winters: cold, dark and long.

X   Xmas: the official home of Santa Claus and Rudolph is in Lapland [Ed: Norwegians in particular will challenge this].

Y   YLE: Finnish Broadcasting Company transmitting daily in English, French and German.

Z   Zoo in Helsinki.

Å   Swedish 'O'. Six per cent of Finns are Swedish speakers.

Ä Ö   Funny Finnish vowels, sometimes transliterated into English as AE or OE. For example *"Älä lyö ääliö"* = "Don't hit me, you jerk". English version: Aelae lyoe aeaelioe.

Many leaders of this early independence movement were severely punished, some by exile. It was a hard time. The Finns did not have the physical means of rejecting Tsarist hegemony and the Russians were increasingly determined not to loosen the ties between the two countries any further.

However, the fortuitous outbreak of the 1917 Russian Revolution gave the Finns the opportunity they needed. Two months after fighting began in Russia, Finland took advantage of the turmoil to declare herself independent - on December 6, which has ever since been designated National Day.

So, after centuries of dominance by Sweden and a pro-longed period under the Tsars, Finland finally became independent. The country's constitution, still largely in force, was signed in 1919 by Lieutenant-General (as he was at the time) Carl Gustav Mannerheim, the towering figure of modern Finland's history.

Tragically, the declaration of independence led directly to a civil war in Finland which reflected the 'Red' versus 'White' confrontation across the Eastern frontier.

The bloody struggle continued from January to May 1918, a conflict which even today is said to have left scars on the nation's psyche. One of the 'ifs' of history is what would have happened to the newly independent Finland if the Finnish 'Reds' had prevailed. But they did not. The 'White' forces, led by Mannerheim, were the victors and temporarily he became the Republic's President, a position he was to hold for a second time in 1944.

Defeated but not occupied

The Finns had a complicated Second World War which put their powers of survival and their *"sisu"* [endurance or 'guts'] to the fiercest of tests.

82

In 1939 the then Soviet Union launched an attack on Finland, precipitating the so-called "Winter War". Hostilities continued for over three months, frequently in temperatures of under -30°C and 100,000 Finns died or disappeared in the conflict. It was an unequal struggle, though the invading forces gravely underestimated the Finns' ferocity and the sinister skills of the guerilla tactics they used under Marshal Mannerheim's command.

In the end the Finns sued for peace, losing Karelia in the process. Some 430,000 Finns fled this agriculturally and historically rich corner of the country and settled further west.

But the country was not occupied by the Russians, an important fact to remember. In 1941 Finland chose to become an ally of Germany when Hitler attacked the Soviet Union. This second involvement in hostilities is known to the Finns as the "Continuation War".

When the tide turned against Germany, the Finnish forces were also evicted from Russia - only to be faced with the problem of dealing with German forces who were in defensive positions in the north of Finland.

Finnish forces were deployed to harass the Germans who retreated through Lapland into Norway, burning everything on their way.

The Treaty of Paris of 1947 fixed Finland's post-war frontiers.

So Finland, along with Great Britain, was the only country not to have been occupied during WWII, a fact in which the Finns still take pride today.

Lapland

One-third of Finland's landmass lies above the Arctic Circle - the wild tundra called Lapland where the few thousand Sami people live, look after reindeer, hunt and fish.

Traditionally nomadic, most of the Samis live these days in well established settlements, snowmobiles parked outside their robust and pretty wooden houses.

In the winter this is a land of endless darkness - apart from the *aurora borealis* - and, in the summer, a land of stinging light which keeps sleep at bay around the clock.

Whichever extremity of the seasons one visits, Lapland is a profoundly affecting country, an experience not to be missed - although few Finns seem to have gone north of Rovaniemi.

This is also dangerous country for the inexperienced. Guides should be used wherever possible. Finnish Lapland is an area with a population of less than ten inhabitants per km2!

The Finnish national anthem includes the words "No valley, no hill, no water, no shore more beloved" which summarise the Finns' relationship to the natural environment. Contrary to popular beliefs, there are valleys and hills in Lapland, as well as water and shores, and the foreigner can best understand the words of the anthem by a visit to the Arctic Circle...

A presidential system

From 1154 to 1809, when she became a Grand Duchy in the Russian empire, Finland was ruled by her neighbour across the Gulf of Bothnia, the Kingdom of Sweden. In 1917 she achieved independence and, after World War II, adopted a policy of neutrality.

There are some similarities between the constitution of the Finnish republic, ratified in July 1919, and the French presidential system. The President, who is directly elected for a maximum of two consecutive six-year mandates, is entrusted with supreme executive power.

The Finnish parliament, a single chamber, comprises 200 members who are elected every four years. The government is formed by the Prime Minister, who is appointed by the President.

The two official languages of the republic are Finnish and Swedish. Titles of nobility were abolished under the new constitution.

After the last war, most Finnish governments seemed to last little more than a year. However the trend in recent years has been towards more durable solutions, mainly coalitions between the Social Democrats and the Conservatives, or between the Social Democrats and the Centre Party.

But Finnish politics remain quarrelsome and insular, striking outsiders as having all the dignity of a fight in a phone-booth, with not much to be won or lost. With 21 registered parties, some of them of eccentric persuasions, political life does indeed have the clamour of a Saturday morning market and, one might add, as much of its relevance.

Nonetheless, a foreigner should be prudent: political 'old boy' networks are everywhere to be found in the country's economic and social life. Job preferment in this hierarchically minded country is frequently done on the basis of party affiliation. This is perfectly understood, even acceptable, and in some cases is the only explanation for an otherwise bizarre choice or appointment.

The complex undercurrents of Finnish political life, as well as the influence they have on the country's economic activity, should be treated with some prudence by others, as they are indeed by the Finns themselves. Old conflicts, the traditional struggle between the rural and the urban, persist with a surprising ferocity and with personal antipathies.

Just as it is unwise to assume in Finland that so-and-so cannot possibly know 'Mr X' or 'Ms Y' (when you will probably find that, worse, they are actually related!), so it is prudent to take silent account of the politics of the situation, precisely because the Finns themselves will not draw attention to this very important aspect of the way they do business with one another. Rightly or wrongly, they take the view that this is nobody else's business.

Yet it has been the very speed of the 'Finnish miracle' - against the backdrop of sullen ambiguities during the Cold War years, as well as the dash from the farmyard to full-scale Nordic welfarism - which explains the fierceness of Finnish politics.

A flair for free trade

Finland's membership of the European Union has put an end to the question which has bedevilled the country's economic and political profile since WWII, namely "where does Finland belong?".

The EU will also help to define what sort of country Finland will be in the future, not least because there will be stronger international confidence in the Finns which, in turn, will help them to solve some of their own problems.

Not that Finland has, as it were, come out of the cold exactly. Finland had been a member of the European Free Trade Association (EFTA) since 1961 and signed a free trade agreement with the EEC, as the Union was known then, in 1973. The country has also been a longstanding member of GATT, the IMF, the World Bank, the Council of Europe and the OECD.

At the end of the last war Moscow imposed a heavy programme of reparations on the Finns. Just about everything which could be moved east was moved, even railway sleepers. It was an extremely hard time for Finland but, ironically, it sowed the seeds of economic recovery.

The Finns had no alternative but to move directly from a semi-agricultural economy to an industrialised one. And this they did with remarkable speed, considering that Finland by choice was not a beneficiary of the Marshall Plan - which means that they did it on their own, within their own resources. In short, a great achievement.

Until the mid-'70s, the economy grew by an average of six per cent per annum and was characterised as a 'little big country', which it still is.

With the exception of the danger posed by the colossal public borrowing debt and structural unemployment, Finland looks forward to the millenium in a reasonably buoyant mood. The rate of investment in R&D is growing steadily and exports of high-tech products have grown faster in recent years than in other industrialised countries.

This is a tribute to the very exacting standards of the country's educational system, especially in the fields of the natural sciences and technology.

The principles of free trade are anything but new to the Finns and their dependence on foreign trade is high, as it is for other 'small' countries. Over 65 per cent of the country's exports go to other EU economies. The Union is also Finland's largest source of imports.

Finnish companies are attempting to revive their traditional trade with Russia, which plummeted after the Soviet Union's collapse. Machinery and equipment is the largest group of products to be exported to Russia, with a fair number of turnkey construction projects in that country. Crude oil and natural gas account for almost half of Russian imports to Finland by value.

The Finns are proud of their expertise in things Russian and see many opportunities for a role in EU-Russian economic cooperation through their country's location and its excellent infrastructure. Finland bills itself as a natural gateway to Russia and of course to the Baltic States.

During the Cold War, the Baltic Sea marked the east-west divide in northern Europe, but those conditions have changed so fundamentally that Finland, like Sweden, sees great commercial possibilities in the altered situation - not only for herself, but also by acting together with companies and interests from other parts of the EU in developing and improving trade with the East.

The Åland Islands

Midway between Finland's original capital, Turku, and Stockholm are the 6,000 Åland Islands which are Swedish-speaking but under Finnish sovereignty. Almost half the Åland's 25,000 population live in the capital, Mariehamn. They enjoy semi-autonomous status and have their own parliament (the *Lagting*) which has legislative competence in many areas, including education, health, industry and the postal service. Young male Ålanders are exempt from the 11-month compulsory Finnish national service.

The islands were the home to many of the Cape Horn 'tall ships' and still have the last remaining vessel to be preserved in its original state. The 'Pommern' lies in Mariehamn's harbour magnificently housing a maritime museum.

Sailing westwards towards the Ålands, through thousands of islands and rock outcrops, is a memorable experience, especially in the summer months. It's also great fun.

All the taxis in Mariehamn have ships' names in place of licence plates. A small flag on the front of the cab stands for the letter 'z' which means 'I need a tug'...

The Finnish world of values

It's a pity but - despite their heroic modern history, their at times adversarial climate and the sleek modernity of a Nordic welfare state - the Finns have a low self-esteem which frequently crystallises in the question of the Finnish 'image'.

Ironically, it was one of the country's most revered 19th-century historians, Zacharias Topelius, who articulated what many still believe are some of the seminal elements of the Finnish psyche, embodied in the traditional character of 'Matti'.

"By nature Matti is not one to get excited.

"He is close-mouthed and shy.

"But when he sits for a time in the company of good friends, he seems to loosen up and undergo a transformation of character, as it were.

"His wooden composure softens, he may even become cheerful and witty in his own way.

"The whole world also knows that Matti is stubborn as sin itself: his immobility is, in fact, the reverse side of his endurance. Whatever he once gets into his head, he will take to its conclusion. Wherever he stands, there he stands; but when he has no will for something, it is simply futile to try to coax him into it."

Is this a caricature? Not entirely, and there are other cultural traits that tend to reinforce the impression that Finns are altogether different. Pertti Widén, head of Turku University of Commerce's Language Department and an expert in intercultural communication, writes:

"Finnish politeness is often passive. Finns avoid calling special attention to a person while, in other cultures, politeness may be active and expressed: they pay specific attention to a person. Finnish politeness is not disturbing a person. That is why Finns do not look at the person, they do not address him directly, they avoid calling him by name."

He goes on: "The Finnish world of values that emphasises individualism and the European that emphasises cooperation may rub one another the wrong way...

"The Finnish lack of body language is also due to the high value placed on verbal communication. While American studies show that words communicate only 7 per cent of the message and the remaining 93 per cent come from gestures and other non-verbal communication, the Finns ignore a large part of this communication resource."

This is in large part why Finns have a reputation for being taciturn and glum. In fact, they do tend to speak when there's something to be said. But, if there's nothing to be said, then silence is not the embarrassment it would be in other cultures - where to have a conversational vacuum is almost social death.

As a consequence of EU membership, large numbers of officials at both national and local levels have been attending crash courses in how to negotiate 'European-style', how to deal with multicultural situations, and even how to make small talk. This is typical of Finnish seriousness: they don't like to chatter - but, very well, they will learn to do it!

In addition, they are undoubtedly a shy people, an attribute which often gives those unused to Finns the impression that they are rude or gauche. But the Finns want to take their time, get used to their interlocutor before they let their guard down. How much time depends on the circumstances, but it can take years. One needs to be as patient as the Finns are themselves, so a first encounter is most unlikely to lead to a social breakthrough. If you like the person, you have to think of the experience in terms of laying down a good wine. It will eventually ripen into something splendid.

As might be imagined, these unfamiliar characteristics can, and do, give rise to many misapprehensions. We have never heard anyone say or write that they don't like Finns, but they do have a tendency to inspire a slightly despairing perplexity - not least in their notorious reluctance to write letters or reply to fax or phone calls, even though it may be keenly in their interest to do so. This is a characteristic they share with the Swedes.

Wild and inaccurate guesses

Because Finland is isolated and therefore a relatively unfamiliar society, it is the victim of wild and inaccurate guesses on the part of foreigners as to the sort of country it might be.

The regular and invaluable *Helsinki Guide* has a standard two pages entitled "Finland - What it is not!" which tackles head-on some of the vulgarities others believe of the country.

For instance, Finland has never been a part of the Eastern Bloc. Finns and Lapps are not the same. Finland is not fearfully cold all the time. It is not a country of limitless sex, and Finns don't drink as much as the rumours suggest (Finland only achieves a fair average, number 23 out of 33 countries).

Drinking comes high on the list of superficial impressions, partly because this is a reputation that the Nordics, like the Irish, cannot shake off. In a list of negatives about Finland drawn up by a management school, "drinking habits" made an inevitable appearance. But wait... a list of Finnish virtues was drawn up at the same time and "drinking habits" was in that column too!

The Finns are 'bout drinkers'. Lengthy periods of abstinence culminate in binges where no bottle is left empty - a throwback to the farmer's weekly visit to market to sell his produce, the only time he had cash in hand.

Such a habit of consumption can obviously lead to disastrous social consequences, later understandingly forgiven, but which give the impression that Finns are in the Olympic Class when it comes to alcohol consumption, which just isn't true. As elsewhere in the Nordic region, the price of drink is set deliberately high as an act of policy to restrain intake.

Certainly the Finns have a taste for the occasionally bucolic, as well as the alcoholic, both in their humour and socialising. Where else would one find such a wonderfully expressive word for a traditional dance as the *"humppa"*? The name itself is enough to set your foot tapping to the accordion.

The Finns are close to nature, and in a more direct way than the Swedes. The country's industrial revolution was post-Second World War, delayed as it was by the need to make reparations to the Soviet Union. Many of those who work in industry are only two generations removed from the land. The country 'cottage' is often the parents' smallholding handed down through the family and transformed into a holiday home for winter, and especially summer, use.

To be perfect, this idyll should be inaccessible by road, have a lake-side sauna, a well, a small boat and some apple trees. It should also have a veranda or terrace, a barbeque, a swing in the garden and a darts board on the outside wall of the woodshed. In the surrounding forest there will be secret places with bountiful supplies of berries and mushrooms.

Such a scene is literally and figuratively the heartland of the Finnish culture - reflecting love of nature, as the Finns put it - and it is here, in the country, that national traditions most clearly reflect Finnish characteristics. Whatever the pleasures of Finnish urban life, the true resilience of the nation's culture lies in the countryside.

No foreigner should pass up the opportunity to visit rural Finland. Solitude and silence are the clues to the Finnish soul, reflected in the old saying that "if one is happy, one must be silent." For the Finn, the proper acknowledgement of joy is silence. For the foreigner, the difficulty is knowing whether silence indicates pleasure or melancholy. A clue is to be found in another Finnish saying: "To be silent is gold, talking is silver."

A more prosaic indication of the need for "aloneness", in the most intimate circumstance, is when a wife greets her spouse in the morning with the words: "Don't kiss me, it's breakfast time"...

Kate Moore, an American academic who teaches linguistics at Helsinki University, summarises Finnish reticence as follows: "To a Finn, English or American politeness seems exaggerated, somewhat fake and even absurdly ritualistic. The Finns, who often opt for avoidance of personal reference or attention, take the opportunity to say nothing and acquiesce as a polite, magnanimous gesture. For example, if a Finn steps in front of a person viewing a painting in a museum, neither party would expect an apology. The English use of 'excuse me' in Finnish would be somewhat odd."

It also has to be remembered that, for a Finn, laughter is not necessarily a social attribute; often the spontaneity of it can be suspect. Is the person drunk or frivolous or both? One often quoted Finnish saying is *"Mies tulee räkänenästäkin, vaan ei tyhjän naurajasta"*. ["Even if your nose is running you're a man - unless you laugh"]. Yes, they appreciate the strong, silent type in Finland.

The emotional magma

There is a certain heartlessness in Finnish attitudes for which the outsider should be ready, if not reconciled to.

The Finns are masters of the casual dismissal, a sort of flip fatalism. Phrases equivalent to "So what?", "Too bad", "Who cares?", "Serves him right", offer culturally different foreigners an unattractive insight to the Finnish character - hinting at putting the other fellow down or reflecting an 'it's-none-of-my-business' attitude. A shrug of the shoulder in Finland can be almost as dismissive as the Gallic version.

And yet finer passions, or at least strongly sentimental ones, lurk below the surface. They can be disguised or dormant for years before a generally ill-timed appearance. More often than not it requires drink or music, preferably both, to cause the emotional magma to break surface and start flowing but, when it does, there are only two possibilities - stand your ground or flee.

Of course this eruption may only be inaccurately recalled the next morning - if at all - and it is best to leave it like that. There's no point in inviting further 'Finnbarrassments'. In any case, there is always the sauna, the tribune of the Finnish psyche, its *sine qua non*, it's be-all-and-end-all.

Where else are habit and necessity so harmoniously combined as in the sauna? In what other way does ritual combine with informality or business with friendship or family with national pride? The Finns have made many contributions to European civilisation, but none as distinctive as the sauna. The trouble is that it is a bit like Italian cuisine - despite its reputation it does not, in truth, travel very well.

The sauna can only be truly appreciated in its land of origin: throw more water on the stones and pass the birch twigs! And outside - best of all - lies the prospect of powdery snow to sting the heat from your steaming skin.

One of the many paradoxes which make the Finns a source of fascination - because the tensions in themselves, and between the rest of the world and themselves, are so clear - is their xenophobia. This can be expressed with alarming candour or done more subtly behind one's back. One of the arguments against EU membership was the threat that also exercises the

Austrians, the Swedes and the Danes, namely that foreigners will come and buy up their country homes. What the Finns forget is that what they take for granted, climatically speaking, others may regard with something like horror.

The foreign takeover of rural Finnish idylls is unlikely to happen, but the fear of it happening remains. In an historical sense, the Finns have always enjoyed privacy and relative isolation, and the fear that this may be about to change is strongly felt, no matter what rational arguments may be deployed.

Fine hosts

Yet - paradox again - the Finns are among the finest hosts anyone could wish for. They know with instinctive competence and grace how to make a visitor welcome. They are shy, but gregarious. They embrace the world, but privately find it wanting by comparison with Finnish concerns and habits.

There is nothing two-faced in this. It's just that they can, and mostly do, live harmoniously with their divided sentiments. Just as the Finns reconcile their deep attachment to the rural aspects of their heritage with the stresses of urban modernity, so they manage to combine a sense of international citizenship with the small parochialisms, tinged with nationalism, of their own blend.

By contrast, the majority of Norwegians have not so far been able to reconcile a similar dichotomy. But the Finns have always had a large and unruly neighbour to the east, one that remains volatile and restive, so that the political advantage of EU membership can be seen with relative clarity.

Still, it may surprise the first-time visitor how little the Finns talk of Russia or have ever been there, even only as far as St Petersburg which is a mere six-hour train ride from Helsinki. In 20 years' journeying to Finland, we have only met two natives who could speak Russian, and one was a Ministry of Foreign Affairs official. Except in the most general terms, the neighbour is not an interest, still less a pre-occupation. For most Finns, Russia is an eternity away and they will never board the shabby green carriages of the St Petersburg express.

Culturally closer and only eighty kilometers south of Helsinki across the Gulf of Finland lies Tallinn, Estonia's capital, with which the Finns are now having much more, and increasing, contact.

The Finns and Estonians can more or less understand what each of them is saying. More or less they like each other - though a certain wariness marks their relations - and trade between the two countries has been increasing sharply.

A trip to Tallinn is, however, to cross a new frontier between Europe's have's and have-not's, between the prim edges of the European Union and the buccaneering capitalism without conscience of the former Communist states. The louche-looking fellow passengers are alone worth the price of the ticket: a wad of dollars in one pocket, a hipflask in another, there is something furtive yet urgent in their manner. Will they, too, in due time become EU citizens?

Midsummer

This is the Big Postponement: Life, Work, Love, Responsibility, even taxes and deadlines, can be put on hold and forgotten in the cathartic celebration of summer.

There really is nothing like it. At this time of year in Finland, they tell you to keep the Champs Elysées, ignore Venice's Grand Canal, shrug at sunset over San Francisco Bay, yawn at Rome's Trevi Fountain.

Infinitely better is the glimpse of the Baltic distantly glittering through the birches, the whiff of woodsmoke and sausage on the wind. See a morning of encroaching mists, feel the weight of fish in the net, hear the watery percussion of the oars of the only boat in the world, as it

---

moves pre-dawn through the islands of the archipelago. Later there will be a sauna, a barbecue under the pines, a sentimental accordion, the concluding smudge of the Midsummer Night sun and the knowledge that day will come again in a few minutes.

Certainty, hope, optimism are suddenly welded as seamlessly as day with day. Do you recall Isak Borg in Bergman's masterpiece "Wild Strawberries"?

"I don't know how it happened," he reflects at a certain moment, "but the day's clear reality changed into the shapes of a dream. I don't even know if it was a dream or if it was memories that appeared with the strength of real events."

And so it is with the Summer Solstice in Finland. Dreams, memories, the present, combine in rich conspiracy to uplift and yet to sadden.

Those voices, clear and sharp across the water, are from the past. Smoke rises from the chimney of a distant farmhouse now occupied by strangers. There used to be a jetty just here, long ago destroyed by the ice, and the dog whose wilful cavortings among the reeds gave such wonderful companionship has been dead these many years. Lift a solemn glass to them all: the 'have-beens', the 'might-have-beens', the full chorus of 'I wish-they-were's'.

The Finns are unashamed of this sentimental interlude. It will be a pleasure not necessarily expressed in laughter (though they hope for that) and not necessarily through a mist of nostalgia (though it is all too likely), but with a contentment which doesn't always call itself happiness but which one knows at a certain age it must be.

Midsummer is the year's most redemptive moment, the benchmark for all the other seasons, the meridian like no other which urges Finns to look back on a whole life's perspective - and forward to its reenactment in many more Midsummers, waking up drunk in a cornfield.

An industrial tripod

The Finnish economy rests on a basic tripod of activities: the traditional one, forestry and high-quality paper and board, the engineering industry and, lastly, a variety of industries like chemicals, textiles, clothing and services. In joining the European Union, it is clear that Finland has major economic interests to protect.

But the national debt also has to be tackled. The OECD estimates that, at current rates, Finland's debt will grow in 30 years to three times GDP! If the country were to continue borrowing at the present rate, all Government revenue would eventually go into debt servicing...

There are few illusions in Finnish industry that the adjustments in economic policy as a result of EU membership will be painful. In particular, agriculture will be in for a hard time. Companies working the domestic market face sharper competition and lower profitability. And - an increasing refrain among both officials and business people - Finland needs more investment, foreign and domestic. Foreigners have often described Finland as 'too small' for investment in the past, but EU membership is confidently expected to bring a change in this traditional attitude.

This is important because, apart from the 'green gold' of forest products, Finland has few national resources and no windfalls such as Norway's North Sea oil and gas.

In the past, Finland was the poorest of the Nordic countries. Some of the attitudes shown towards the Finns by the Swedes, Danes and Norwegians derive from this history. Linguistically, too, the Finns are 'the odd ones out'.

But matters have changed dramatically in the last fifty years. Professor W R Mead puts it succinctly in his recent book, 'An Experience Of Finland': "The advance from penury to prosperity is an experience in which two generations of Finns have shared. A third generation, born to high expectations, may have difficulty in maintaining the rate of development. Compensatingly, it is unlikely that the present generation of Finns will have to deal with problems equal in magnitude to those that have confronted their parents and grandparents."

Today's youngsters may face the problem of not being able to find their first job in Finland on the completion of their education or training. Emotionally, they will be uneasily poised between their strong sense of identity and the need for work. A diaspora across the Union of talented Finns of both sexes is in prospect. They have the skills, the languages and the enterprise to seek work outside their country - and may have to. Structural unemployment could be the modern equivalent of a potato famine in moving people out and away.

Even so, as Finland moves towards a post-industrial society, she does so with confidence and in the certainty that she is making the right choices. From an economy which was historically based on primary products and their refinement, the country has turned towards the logical next stage of high technology.

Growth in Finnish high-tech products was among the OECD's fastest during the '80s and more recently accounted for 16 per cent (and rising) of exports.

The Technical Research Centre of Finland is the largest such institute in the Nordic area. Cooperation between industry, the universities and research organisations is as intimate and mutually sustaining as anywhere in the European Union.

In this respect the Finns have a clear vision of where they need to go - and how to get there. R&D is the basis of that vision.

We think of Goethe's Faust:

"Are you in earnest? Seize this very minute.
What you can do, or dream you can, begin it.
Courage has genius, power and magic in it.
Only engage, and then the mind grows heated,
Begin it, and the work will be completed."

The Finns are in earnest, right enough. Too 'blue-eyed' (innocent) sometimes, too keen on false economies, too stubborn, too modest, dare one even say too honest? But when they match ambition and discipline with technology and commercial acumen, they are formidable.

Yet they can be disconcertingly easy to underestimate, because they do not present themselves in the way others expect, and this is particularly so of their educational standards which are amongst the highest in Europe. The pressure on schoolchildren and students for academic achievement is enormous. And, in a society where income has little to do with status, it is learning - or lack of it - which often makes for invidious social distinctions.

Lack of continuity

It is something of a shock in a society with strongly held egalitarian values to hear someone sneeringly put down on account of his or her lack of tertiary education. Yet if they have other achievements to their names, these can be derided as fortuitous or second-rate. It's rather sad, as is the wastefulness with which achievers become non-persons the moment midnight strikes on the last day of their professional lives. Accumulated wisdom, long and expensively bought experience, count for nothing any more. Continued participation in

The Age of the Engineer

When he wakes up, the shrewd 'dinosaur' asks himself two questions. First: am I extinct? Second: if not, how long have I got?

Of course it is an exaggeration to compare this creature with today's Finnish businessman, but a similar lack of confidence is apparent in Finland.

It is true that the style of industrial and commercial leadership has changed markedly since the '70s and early-'80s. Just as well, since there was a buccaneering spirit then - or at least the semblance of such a spirit - that would be completely inappropriate in today's conditions.

Furthermore, the strange *nouveau riche* suits - the ones with lurex threads in them - which were so popular in those boisterous days have been discarded in favour of technocrats' greys and dark blues. There are no regrets about that either.

But, timely though it is in many respects, the "Age of the Engineer" in Finnish management - as they choose to call it - has been marked by a drop in self-esteem. The leadership of Finnish industry is these days making a virtue out of mediocrity.

Could it be that the '70s and early-'80s were not really to do with absolutes of management competence at all? Is it possible that in the circumstances of those days, the things Finland was best at exporting - the forest and engineering industries' products - commanded world prices which were extremely favourable to the country?

Was it also at just the same period that Finland was able to buy imports which, relatively speaking, were inexpensive to the nation?

The answer in both cases is 'yes'. And this being the case, these boom years could have much more to do with external factors than with invincible Finnish management skills, of which there is not much so evidence in the '90s. Indeed, were those skills an illusion?

What has happened in the past few years is that the situation has reversed: Finnish exports now command less, while the bill for imports is growing. Competition will also increase with the country's accession to the EU.

Certainly a gloomy mood about the economy is a commonplace. The aspiration of management seems to be to take a decision not to take a decision...

Not taking decisions, putting everything on hold, may give a superficial appearance of sagacity, but is nothing of the kind. It's the Nordic version of "mañana".

In the '80s, Finland was often called the "Japan of the North" (of which one academic rightly said that anyone using the phrase understood neither Finland nor Japan).

For the '90s, what next?

It's time to ask the 'dinosaur' questions, but these days few are inclined to indulge in self-examination in a country which has been so battered by recession.

old sauna or hunting clubs may be tolerated, but that tends to emphasise the abrupt divide between those now in charge and yesterday's man.

"I'm very glad you spoke to me", a veteran industrialist leaning on his walking stick said during a chance encounter in a shopping mall. The implication was clear: as he had retired, few would speak to him any more...

While there is every reason for older business leaders to move over for the coming generation, the lack of a sense of continuity means that mistakes are often repeated as the new-comers struggle to reinvent the wheel. It is astonishing to see how the management cadres of some Finnish high-tech industries are composed entirely of men and women in their 30s. This trend is helping to break down the hierarchy and for-malism that used to bedevil many of the larger organisations, but it has its downside as well.

Finnish business still shows lingering signs of German influence in terms of hierarchical attitudes and an emphasis on formal educational standards. According to ethnologist Kati Laine-Sveiby, who has made a comparative study of Finnish and Swedish management styles, "the power in the Finnish companies shows a more formal, bureaucratic face. The power distance is more easily to be recognised." Authority, she says, is more demonstratively communicated outward. By comparison, the Swedish executive is trained to understate his authority by a more informal and smoother style, something that Finns can interpret as 'manipulation'.

In contrast, Dr Laine-Sveiby finds that the Finns have a shorter planning perspective than the Swedes and, more-over, regard this as evidence of greater flexibility. Faced with the choice between consensus management techniques and rapid decision-making, the Finns favour the latter. They appreciate 'hands-on' management and qualities like dyna-mism and 'drive'.

In a study undertaken for the Finnish Institute of Management, Professor Andrew Kakabadse and associates from the UK's Cranfield School of Management talk of the "concentration of boardroom power in Finnish industry" and of a tradition of employee loyalty reflected in "a high degree of job mobility within a single organisation." Kati Laine-Sveiby also found that job rotation was valued by Finnish management.

The Cranfield report goes on to comment that "if anyone adopts too individualistic a style, then he or she is likely to have an adverse impact on the generation of and commitment to implementing strategies for the future." And, further on: "Development in entrepreneurial skills and ways of working may be an important need for Finnish managers working for multinationals in fast-evolving market conditions."

The Cranfield study concludes that the capacity of Finnish executives "to manage difficulties, sensitivities and different contingencies is high." Such human qualities extend, as one might expect of countries with a tradition of consensus, to Finland's Nordic neighbours: "There is a greater preponderance of effective communication and delegation and higher levels of managerial maturity among Finnish and Swedish top managers than among most others in Europe."

A Finnish epilogue

We were going to write "in conclusion...", but there is no conclusion. A Finnish MP commented recently that the less written about his country by outsiders, the better - which certainly illuminates the atavism that is so much a part of the Finnish character. If they could, most Finns would really like to close the door on the rest of the world. They remain ambivalent about this emotional need for isolation and the other imperatives which are symbolised by EU membership.

In many ways Finland is the most exotic, and certainly the least known, of the new EU entrants and it cannot quite make up its mind whether it wishes to remain so or not. For purely geographic reasons, it probably will - and this is ultimately no bad thing. A certain mysteriousness always hovers in the margins of contact with the Finns and their country. It is part of their charm and fascination that nothing is entirely all it seems: what is not said or done in Finland is often much more interesting than what is. Foreigners should remember this.

And there are plenty of paradoxes. The Finns have fierce honesty yet, in contrast to their Swedish neighbours, their instincts are on the side of non-disclosure, if not secrecy. They are shy, but wonderfully convivial: they want to be private but take a confident place in a wider world.

There are all the clichés, many of them shared with the Swedes: the country's scenic beauty, crayfish, the taste for strong coffee, the ubiquitous tango rhythms of the accordions, candles burning in daylight, overheated interiors (during winter), the obsession with sports, Europe's most diligent reading habits, Sibelius, the world-famous austerity of design and architecture, the national epic of the Kalevala, the colossal breakfasts, Santa Claus (also claimed to be a native son by Finland's two Nordic neighbours!), Moomin, Baltic herring, the passion for dried flowers, choral singing, those fiercesomely early mornings and late, late nights and, of course, the sauna.

Finland will reward with all of these, but will still remain elusive. Literally and figuratively, she is the European Union's final frontier and will remain so in all her richness. By doing so, she offers so much from which the rest of us can learn – above all, how to be resilient.

The
NewComers

NewComers
NewComers
NewComers
NewComers
NewComers
NewComers
NewComers

Sweden

Distant Sweden

If, seen from the viewpoint of other Europeans, the Austrians are immersed in ignorance and the Finns clouded in mystery, then the Swedes are buried in misconceptions.

Not surprisingly perhaps since Sweden is a country where doors open outwards, bread has sugar in it, a free glass of water is served with every meal, parents are punishable by law for smacking their children, and cars drive around in broad daylight with their headlights blazing.

Of the three countries joining the Union, Sweden is the largest, the wealthiest and, with 8.7 million inhabitants, the most populous. Also, despite the lack of the east-west pivotal position that the other two enjoy, it is the most influential diplomatically.

But the country has inherited an image problem, a massive accretion of misconceptions.

Many foreigners think that all Swedes look the same, flaxen-haired and gangling. Not so. Without taking into account the 10 per cent of the population that is now non-Swede, there are as many dark-haired people, medium-height or even small, as there are blond giants.

But even more bizarre are misconceptions about the psychology and lifestyle of the Swedes.

Some people think of Sweden as a country that refuses to commit itself - despite the fact that, with its decision to join the Union, it has shown that indeed it can. Its history of neutrality and non-intervention has left a more lasting impression on western minds than Austria's.

Others think of Sweden, rightly, as a social laboratory but then go on, wrongly, to equate this with permissiveness and lax morals. Even if the tales of *au pair* girls are true, Swedish sexuality seems pretty tame by today's standards, when you compare this Lutheran people with a Catholic country like Spain. In the words of the country's leading sociologist, Professor Åke Daun, "sexuality has been 'dedramatised', emptied of its earlier cultural and emotional content." Permissiveness reflects the emphasis placed on rationality.

Then there are some of us who, unduly influenced at an impressionable age by Ingmar Bergman's films, are still intrigued by what we see as a cultural dichotomy: a genteel veneer of exquisite taste and gracious living superimposed on a bucolic and colourful culture epitomised in the little red horses of Dalarna.

All of these misconceptions have their roots in reality, yet they are still misconceptions. Sweden is indeed a country that generally keeps out of trouble but it has been doing so instinctively, with the notable exception of the Thirty Years' and the Great Northern wars, since the age of the Vikings.

Sweden has indeed been a social laboratory and it has been so for just as long... and maybe already was in the age of the Vikings. Yet it is not as permissive as others would think, if you can believe the traditional Nordic *bon mot*: "In Sweden everything is prohibited that is not permitted. In Norway everything is permitted that is not prohibited. In Denmark..."

As for the charge of gracious living, the country does indeed still show traces of the 'Bergman veneer'. Bergman was depicting the Stockholm bourgeoisie of his youth, strongly influenced by a French culture imported by Gustav III - but these traces are increasingly thin as they give way to a more homogeneous culture which shows a strong and even growing attachment to the little horses of Dalarna.

All the most persistent misconceptions start from the fact that the Swedes are a naturally democratic people: it is evident at many crucial events in the country's history. They have democracy built into them from birth, or even before. And our misconceptions take root precisely because the rest of us Europeans find it difficult to believe this. Sometimes we are even driven to mistrust Swedish motives.

Where the Finns repress - or occasionally express - their feelings, the Swedes seem to sublimate them. Some innate sense of caution, which helped them avoid major social conflict over the centuries, is now highly developed in the individual and institutionalised in the state. They are mutually reinforcing.

Of course some countries resent people who are so eminently sensible, which only helps to fuel the misconceptions.

Take the metro (the *T-bana*, the 'T' standing for tunnel) northwards from the centre of Stockholm and you could be excused for thinking that you are being given a lesson in Swedish upward mobility.

As you exit the central area, you reach 'Stadion' [Stadium]: this, you conclude, is the mecca of the masses though, as it happens, the masses go there to watch athletics and the popular Swedish variant of ice hockey, *bandy*, rather than football. In the words of a Swedish fan, "when you've got *bandy*, you don't need football." He also says it is the bandy supporters - most of them living in the northern half of Sweden and recognisable by their briefcases laden with *brännvin*-containing coffee called *kask* - who voted against accession to the European Union.

One stop further up the line and you move educationally and socially upwards at a station with the romantic name of 'Tekniska Högskolan' [Technical High School]. And one station further you have the self-explicit 'Universitet'.

Many things in Sweden will remind the foreigner of this country's sometimes frustrated urge to provide better opportunities for all.

Frustration is indeed the 'flavour of the decade', as the country copes with rising unemployment and the government searches for cuts in social expenditure to balance the national budget. Industry, spurred on by the devaluation of the krona in November 1992, is now faring well again but the outlook for the average Swedish family, compared with the glorious '80s, is bleak.

"There is somebody out of work in almost every family, a traumatic experience for people who have taken full employment for granted for the last fifty years", comments a government official. "It was almost exotic to know someone who was unemployed - and a disgrace for the person concerned." The Skogslänen, the forest counties of northern Sweden have always suffered from endemic unemployment but, in the south, it was rare.

Neutrality, not isolationism

Sweden's reasonable approach to solving society's ills goes back to at least the middle of the last century, if not earlier.

The result today is a country which has resolved most of the major issues that other European societies are still grappling with but - to the surprise of some and the *Schadenfreude* of others - is now paying the price. This must give great satisfaction to people like Auberon Waugh.

Sweden pioneered the *ombudsman* concept, an institution which dates back to 1809. There are now six such offices: the parliamentary *ombudsman*, four government-appointed *ombudsmän* responsible respectively for consumer matters, equal opportunities, ethnic discrimination and children's interests, and a press *ombudsman*.

The country also instituted the principle of making all official governmental correspondence available for inspection on request by the media or the public. An ordinary citizen can check the Prime Minister's mail and the popular press is even known to ask to see ministers' expense reports when they suspect abuse of public funds. There are no grounds for denying such requests unless primarily issues of security or foreign relations are involved.

With such a tradition it is hardly surprising that, in the negotiations for accession to the EU, Swedish representations on the need for greater openness in government were particularly lively. Another matter, of great importance to younger Swedes who are trying to kick the smoking habit, was the issue of *snus* [wet snuff].

Sweden is also a pioneer in the creation of equal opportunities for women. At the time of writing, 44 per cent of the members of the Swedish parliament and half the cabinet are female, exceeding the figures for both Finland and Norway. Swedish feminists tend to be less militant than others, having achieved a respectable status in society, but activists are vigilant in ensuring that quotas are respected.

One of the hottest topics of the Cold War was Sweden's apparent pioneering of 'The Third Way': it was more apparent than real because it was a natural extension of the social course the country had embarked on in the 19th century.

Many western European nations resented what they saw as the moralising attitude of Swedes in vaunting the virtues of the 'Swedish Model' and spearheading Europe's halting social missionary work in the Third World.

Swedes will tell you that it was the others who took such an intense interest in what they were doing. They regret the fact that they earned an image as Europe's 'do-gooders'.

They would prefer to practise neutrality in international imagery as much as in international defence...

Neutrality, however, has not meant isolationism or even insularity as a culture. Throughout history, since the time of the Vikings (who, parenthetically, did not wear silly hats), Sweden has been open to the rest of the world and has maintained contact - sometimes aggressively, more often peacefully - with the other peoples of Europe. The country's accession to the EU is a natural conclusion to a long chapter of European history.

From German merchants to Greek restaurants

The roster of valuable immigrants to Sweden includes German merchants trading through the Hanseatic League, Finnish pioneers, Walloon ironsmiths (who went on to achieve managerial and even ministerial rank), Dutch merchants, Scots mercenaries, German engineers, even a French general who was 'headhunted' for the throne. In the 16th century more than half the population of Stockholm was foreign.

The French influence was most evident under the rule of Gustav III who, at the end of the 18th century, came under the spell of the 'Enlightenment' and imported ideas, fashions, playwrights, artists and architects from Paris. It is this influence, particularly in Gustaviansk architecture and furniture, that comes through in the films of Ingmar Bergman. But it also manifests itself in the rationalism that is the leitmotiv of Swedish society.

This French influence was supplanted, in the 19th century, by a German influence encouraged by the rational and highly organised example of the Kingdom of Prussia. "We are Germans in reserve", says a leading Swedish industrialist. "Yet", he concludes, "we differ in our attitude towards 'instructions from above'. Only if we're motivated will we make something work. If we're not, we won't."

Today, the strongest foreign influences are evident in the catering trade. Restaurants offering traditional Swedish cuisine, simple and wholesome, have given way to French bistros and Italian pizzerias (though the Italians have now sold out to Tunisians and Turks, and moved upmarket).

It is a sobering experience to venture into a forest-encircled town in the heart of Sweden and find that the only food available is either French, Italian, Greek or Maghrebian. Even the town of Piteå close to the Arctic Circle has two purportedly French restaurants facing one another in the main street. One, called 'Le Montmartre', is run by a Tunisian. The other, 'Le Pigalle', by an Algerian.

The democratic instinct

Like Austria, Sweden has a proud imperial past, though of shorter duration. There the similarity ends, for the Swedes have had much longer to recover from their post-imperial trauma. They relinquished such ambitions in 1814 and thereby laid the foundations for a policy of peaceful neutrality which has assured them a relatively serene 20th century.

Where Austria has been marked by corporatism as the only practical solution to the troubled times of the first half of the century, Sweden has been slowly evolving a pluralistic society since the mid-1800s. By the turn of this century there were signs of popular activism which would do credit to any country today.

It is as if today's Swedes have a democratic instinct inside them that functions like a gyroscope, keeping their minds and values on a level flightpath.

Many Swedes will tell you, with great conviction, that this democratic instinct has been evident throughout their country's recorded history. Yet Professor Daun suggests that the objective and rational approach they apply to society's problems is perhaps no older than 50 years.

Foreigners puzzling over the country's democratic instincts will be more inclined to think of the Vikings who, from their point of view as foreigners, represent something of an entirely different kind. Yet the story goes that, when the Vikings besieged Paris before becoming 'Normans', the Frankish commander had great difficulty negotiating with them because he couldn't fathom the hierarchy: they were all free men, so they had no leader in the French sense. Things haven't changed all that much since!

At least it can be said that the Vikings ploughed (hacked?) a fairly steady course for a couple of centuries. They only really got a bad press when they started plundering the monasteries. Popular theory would have it that their excursions were prompted by population growth, but more weight can be attached to the fact that it coincided with the abandonment of Mediterranean trade routes at the time of Arab expansion.

Swedish Vikings navigated Russia's rivers to the Black Sea and the Caspian, and are reputed to have bequeathed their hallmark [*rus* = red-headed] to the Russians. They were as fast on their feet and with their horses, which they carried on board their longships, as they were with their oars.

From the time of the Vikings until the middle of the last century, Swedish history looks like a constitutional seesaw with Crown and aristocracy (and latterly government) continually challenging one another's authority. This did indeed prevent any single faction from getting the upper hand for too long, but the frequent contention by Swedes that, when challenged, those in power conceded defeat voluntarily and peacefully is not entirely borne out by the facts.

Sweden has as many bloodstains on its dynastic history as any other European country. Two of its greatest kings - Karl XII and Gustav III - were assassinated, the latter at a masked ball in his own opera house. The country's involvement in the 30 Years' War and the Great Northern War that followed was marked by a barbarity rivalling that of the Vikings. According to a Dutchman who travelled through the country in the early 18th century: "Nowhere in Sweden did I see a single young man between 20 and 40 years of age, only soldiers. The cruel war had swept away almost the entire youth of this unhappy realm... The whole kingdom to an unbelievable degree [has] run to seed."

And yet, nobler impulses shine through from time to time as portents of what was to come. In 1319, in what has been called Sweden's 'Magna Carta', the aristocracy swore absolute fealty to the new King Magnus Eriksson in exchange for his undertaking not to imprison anyone without due examination and judgment under the laws of the time. In 1655 the governor of the Swedish colony on the Delaware river rejected what he described as a 'despicable' proposal from his Dutch neighbours to wage common war on the Indians. In 1788 Swedish officers challenged a royal decision to mount an attack on Russia as 'unconstitutional'.

Living at peace

With the notable exception of the 17th century wars, much of Sweden's history has been lived at peace. For ordinary people, the only 'enemy' was the state itself and, even then, the population understood the values of loyalty and obedience. Sovereignty was synonymous with the freedom to advance your own interests within the context of community well-being. The 'Swedish Model' ultimately represented two not always compatible interests: economic growth on the right, social redistribution of this wealth on the left. It is this combination of demands that has produced today's dilemma.

Evidence of Swedish society's respect for the rights of ordinary people, particularly vis-a-vis the aristocracy, crops up regularly in the country's history. Compared with almost all other European countries, Sweden has always had a much higher percentage of peasant-proprietors. Even in the 16th century, 45 per cent of farmers owned their own land - though the situation was to change drastically for the worse with the population explosion of the 19th century, when nearly 350,000 Swedes left for America and elsewhere.

Feudalism, in the continental European sense, was largely unknown in large areas of Sweden outside the southern provinces under Danish rule and some areas around Lake Mälaren in the centre of the country - areas which were fertile enough to permit the emergence of large estates. Peasants, if they did not like the landowner they worked for, were free to move elsewhere since serfdom was unknown. It was this, as much as anything else, that contributed to the Swedes' innate sense of democracy and self-esteem.

Land ownership was an issue that cropped up regularly throughout Swedish history. The 'Great Reduction' of the late-1600s reduced the aristocracy's share of the land, much of it forest, mainly to the benefit of the Crown. Much of this land was then allotted to officers in the country's armed forces for use in peacetime. But, in addition to buying land from the aristocracy, peasant farmers were able to purchase any Crown property they were cultivating at favourable prices. The result was that, by 1800, peasant-owned land represented over 50 per cent of the total exploitable surface of the country.

Emboldened by the convictions of the Age of Enlightenment and the French Revolution, and the example of a Swedish nobleman with the very unSwedish name of Rutger Maclean, the country embarked on two consecutive reorganisations of peasant land. These, the *Enskiftet* and the *Storskiftet*, were enforced in the late-1700s with the aim of modernising the country's farming industry. The traditional strip-farming system was abandoned to create individual lots of arable and grazing land.

In the 19th century the government took the ultimate step of decreeing total consolidation of properties, the *Laga skiftet*, leading to the typical Swedish landscape of today with its widely scattered farmsteads.

These radical land reforms, rigorously enforced by government, enhanced peasant productivity but inevitably destroyed villages and disrupted community life. In fact land reform, emigration and industrialisation combined to create a process of social disintegration in late-19th century Sweden.

Sweden became a nation, in the opinion of constitutional specialist Professor Olof Ruin, during the reign of Gustav Vasa in the early-16th century. And it was the emergence of parliamentary government during the so-called 'Age of Freedom' in the 18th century that helped the Swedish democratic spirit to develop.

One practical expression was the promulgation of Europe's first Freedom of the Press Act in 1766. This and related developments encouraged the French historian and sociologist Montesquieu to comment that "the beginning of freedom in Europe, and all freedom to be found among men, is to be found in Scandinavia."

Not unlike the current British system, but consistently enhanced in the 19th and 20th centuries, parliament languished under two kings: Gustav III (1771-1792), who opted for a system of absolute monarchy for which he lost his life, and Karl XIV Johan (1818-1844), the ex-general from Napoleon's army whose kingship drove any egalitarian impulses out of his head. He did however, uncharacteristically, improve further on the Freedom of the Press Act. He also had the unpleasant experience, for an elitist Frenchman, of having parliamentarians laugh at him when he tried to give his first - and only - speech in Swedish.

Karl XIV Johan's successor, Oskar I (1844-1859), had similarly authoritarian instincts. But he put them to better use by promoting the care of the poor, prison reform, equal rights for women and the abolishment of the unduly restrictive guild system.

The shaping of society

S weden is unusual among European countries in having already developed a centralised state administration in the 16th and 17th centuries, a process initiated by Gustav Vasa and extended by Axel Oxernstierna who was himself a functionary.

One of the things on which most Swedes agree today is that the country owes the continuance of its democratic traditions to the existence of "a decent political class." As in other countries the criticism, if there is any, is most marked in the younger generations.

Any inclination by politicians to veer from the straight and narrow is inhibited by the mechanisms of open government, in particular the *ombudsman* system and the principle of public access to all official documents other than those relating to national security, foreign affairs or personal records. "This makes everyone aware that they are operating in the public eye", says a senior ministry of justice official. "It encourages efficiency and the fair treatment of every case."

Cabinet ministers are anxious to avoid any impression that they consider themselves different from the people they represent. They address their constituents - and expect to be addressed by them - with the familiar *du*. As a senior businessman puts it, "there is no possibility for a Swedish politician to think he is someone special."

He should have added "she". A female member of the cabinet (currently every other minister is a woman) habitually cycles from her home to the local railway station, takes the commuter train into Stockholm and walks from the central station to her office.

Though security has been tightened since the assassination of Olaf Palme, there is still a tradition of 'government by walking about'. Where the British Chancellor of the Exchequer poses with his little red case in front of No 11 Downing Street and then plunges into a waiting limousine, the Swedish Finance Minister walks down the Drottningsgatan to parliament with his budget papers, tied with a coloured ribbon, in his hands. Everyone tries, despite difficult circumstances, to minimise the distance between government and the governed.

The political reality is that ministers and under-secretaries of state change with changes in governing parties - and this practice has extended recently to advisors and press secretaries. Parliamentary committees, including the one advising on European Union affairs, are particularly powerful.

Sweden enjoys a positive and stable bureaucratic tradition dating back to the reforms of the great statesman Axel Oxenstierna in the early-17th century. Officials are empowered to take decisions, but are fully accountable for them. Ministries are comparatively small by the standards of many other European countries. Much of the implementation is delegated, without right of interference, to government agencies.

The naive foreigner might be forgiven for thinking that, after decades of peaceful coexistence between Swedish government and big business, and with such a sensible and cut-and-dried approach to running a country, the government/industry interface would be frictionless. Yet a senior industrialist insists there is a 'wall' between the two estates of industry and government: "Our public administrations are competent and fully prepared to act on behalf of Swedish industrial interests, but our business people want nothing to do with them."

A senior ministry official insists that the problem goes further: "There are two elite careers for the educated and ambitious Swede: business or public service. Over the years

Social Democrat thinking has created a distinctive culture, and industry keeps its distance. There is even a problem in the public sector. Ministries tend to remain self-sufficient and anonymous, creating another 'wall' between them and the much larger agencies that implement the policies."

An important feature of Swedish public life which goes back hundreds of years at the village level, and is as strong as ever today, is provided by the largely self-motivated and self-motivating interest or activist groups *[folkrörelse]*. The tradition originally established by the *byalag*, the village councils, extended in the mid-19th century to other aspects of public life: the Free Church congregations, the temperance reformers, the Cooperative movement, the trade unions, the sports movement and, latterly, the consumerist movement.

Following a largely unsuccessful government programme in the 1970s to encourage people to move south, the *folkrörelse* tradition has been given further momentum by an organisation called the *Folkrörelserådet*, which finances projects aimed at preserving community life in the provinces under the slogan *"Hela Sveriga ska leva"* ["The whole of Sweden shall live"].

Although Sweden thus shares a corporatist tradition with Austria, the Swedish version differs from the Austrian in projecting grassroots attitudes more than making decisions for the constituencies represented. Yet these activist movements are extremely, perhaps disproportionately, influential. In the words of one Swede, "parliament has a lot of religious people, a lot of non-drinking people. It is not representative of the public..."

In 1981, 32 per cent of the adult population participated in study circles covering such varied subjects as bookbinding, ceramics, Chinese cooking, languages, personal development and even labour market legislation. Local cultural associations also proliferate. "We like the memories and artifacts of the past without being exaggeratedly proud of our culture" says Åke Daun, who also points out that the tradition of such voluntary organisations has had an enormous impact on the structural development of Swedish society.

Sweden has acted as the world's conscience on many aspects of global affairs, in particular by providing aid to developing countries and financial support for, and active participation in, the work of international agencies.

In its own immediate theatre, the country has been a vigorous member of the Nordic Council (the other members are Norway, Finland, Denmark and Iceland), setting an example to the rest of Europe with the establishment of a common labour market as long ago as 1954 and the abolition of passport controls within the area in 1957.

Sweden's accession to the European Union automatically implied fundamental changes in the country's relationship to the rest of the world and not just towards fellow-members of the Nordic Council. An ad hoc committee chaired by Professor Ruin was established to determine the constitutional implications of EU membership. This identified areas where European law would prevail and concluded that explicit reference had to be made in the Swedish constitution to the transfer of certain powers to Brussels.

One of the major subjects of negotiation on accession was the principle of transparency, with the Swedish government defending the practice of making official documents, including EU papers, available for public scrutiny.

The question of EU accession was put to the vote through a national referendum which produced a majority in favour of 52.3 per cent (compared with 66.4 per cent in Austria and 56.9 per cent in Finland). This was the fifth referendum in the country's history. Although, in the words of Olof Ruin, "they are a brutal kind of decision-making", referenda are likely to become a more frequent feature of the Swedish scene.

Perhaps the most famous previous referendum was that of 1955, when the Swedish people rejected the idea of changing over to driving on the right. Eleven years later, the government defied the people's preference and made the change in any case. Despite some anxious moments this went smoothly, largely thanks to a very thorough public information campaign.

Sweden's original parliament, established in 1435, comprised four chambers representing the 'estates' of the nobility, the burgers, the priesthood and the peasantry. This was replaced in 1866 by a two-chamber parliament, with the first chamber consisting of people elected by the county councils *(län)*. This, in turn, was superseded in 1971 by a single chamber of 349 members elected by proportional representation, with a threshold of only four per cent.

While, compared with a country like Austria, Sweden is traditionally a highly centralised country, a growing degree of autonomy is now accorded to local and regional administrations - prompted partly by the need to relieve pressure on the national budget!

This trend has gone hand-in-hand with a rationalisation of the administrative infrastructure: from over 2,000 in the 1950s, the number of communes and municipalities has fallen to some 300. The county councils *(landstingen)* are largely responsible for public health and, to a lesser extent, transport. The communes now have responsibility for the application of both social legislation and local taxation.

Deregulation, decentralisation

Higher education was the subject of a major reform that came into effect in 1993. The new deregulated system is designed to offer greater autonomy to the institutions involved and greater individual choice to the students. Currently more than 30 per cent of upper secondary school leavers go on to university within the following five years. There are three types of general degree: diploma or certificate (*högskole-examen*) after two years' study, bachelor's degree (*kandidat-examen*) after three years, and master's degree (*magister-examen*) after four years.

Sweden has seven central government-operated universities: Uppsala, Lund, Gothenburg, Stockholm, Umeå in the north, Linköping, and the University of Agricultural Sciences near Uppsala. In addition there are four major specialised institutions: the Karolinska Institute (medicine), the Royal Institute of Technology, Luleå University College and Institute of Technology in the far north, and the Stockholm Institute of Education. All these institutions provide research and development facilities for industry, with Lund University offering valuable support to Sweden's dynamic health care industry.

More than 50 other smaller universities and colleges are located throughout the country. Because of the remoteness of many communities from the main centres, particularly in the north, distance learning is also an important aspect of Swedish education.

Another significant feature is adult education. About half of the country's adult population pursues studies in one form or another. Such a high proportion can only be explained, at least in part, by the longstanding tradition of studies established by the *folkrörelse* movements.

English is now taught in all Swedish schools from the age of eleven, with German or French the second language. In the 19th century the French language and culture were the principal choice of the Swedish bourgeoisie. French then gave way slowly to German and, by the early-1900s, most families professed German as their first foreign language.

By any standards, the Swedes are a well-educated people. It is all the more surprising that some of them demonstrate a marked lack of interest in, or familiarity with, features of their own country and society.

Improvements in the country's already overworked transportation infrastructure are a priority concern with Sweden's accession to the European Union. Industry, all too aware of the country's peripheral location, looks for improvements but is reluctant to share the financial burden. Lack of funds and environmental concerns have hindered development of the modest motorway network and the modernisation of trunk roads. Maybe the authorities had this in mind when, in 1977, they introduced the requirement to use headlights in daytime - a measure that has led to a 10 per cent reduction in collisions between oncoming traffic.

The most positive transport initiatives are the upgrading of main rail links for both high-speed trains (the ABB X2000) and high-capacity freight traffic, and the construction of the Öresund bridge link between Malmö and Copenhagen. Rail track and train services are run as separate operations.

The country is well endowed with telecommunications systems, boasting the world's second highest ownership of telephones (the highest being Monaco) and one of the fastest growth rates for sales of personal computers. Twelve per cent of Swedes and over 20 per cent of Stockholmers have mobile phones.

Sweden has had a housing policy since the 1930s depression, with non-profit municipal housing companies now owning about 50 per cent of all rented apartments in the country. Total accommodation is about four million units, of which slightly over half are in blocks of apartments. Approximately 30 per cent of Sweden's total population live in the three metropolitan areas of Stockholm, Gothenburg and Malmö.

Swedish TV and radio is currently in a state of flux. While the Nordic Council would like to create a common programme for all member countries, Sweden is facing up to deregulation and the inroads of commercial broadcasters. One of the hopefully permanent features of the Swedish TV scene is a mime called Roger, who has a slot on Channel 1 breakfast TV: his audience is children, but he entrances adults just as readily.

In early-1995 there were four Swedish TV transmitters: Channel 1 which is a national service, Channel 2, also state-controlled, which has the task of representing the rest of the country (40 per cent of its programmes are regionally oriented), Channel 3 which is a satellite-transmitted commercial programme, and Channel 4 which is a land-based commercial programme. Cable networks are growing fast: by 1992, these already covered 45 per cent of Swedish households.

State TV and radio have strict instructions on respecting minority interests, whether they happen to be audiences in the remoter areas of the country or minority groups in the cities. Radio services include programmes for the Sami (Lapps) and the Finnish-speaking minorities, as well as services in Albanian, Arabic, Greek, Iranian, Polish, Serbo-Croat, Slovene, Spanish, Syrian and Turkish.

Sweden, perhaps not surprisingly as a well educated and articulate country, comes close to having the world's highest per capita consumption of newspapers: over 90 per cent of the population read at least one daily paper. Swedish law explicitly prohibits the investigation or disclosure of a journalist's sources.

One last word on the media scene. One of the great institutions in Sweden, as in Finland, is 'Kalle Anka' - none less than Donald Duck. Over one million copies of this cartoon weekly are bought by Swedes and fellow-Nordics, young and old. Its parent magazine in the US sells only 40,000...

The art of living

Depending on where you come from, there's a fair chance you will perceive the Swedes as sullen, awkward, proud or permissive - or all of these things. In every case you will be wrong.

The minority makes the stereotype - in this case, with the help of Bergman's films, that of 'The Gloomy Swede'. Apart from the stories told about the Swedish Americans of Minnesota, there are so many myths.

"We are a very serious people," says a senior foreign affairs official rather severely, "we take things seriously." Indeed the Swedes are a serious people, which is a long way from saying that they lack a sense of humour. It's just that, when a subject is serious, it is addressed seriously.

"Yet we are very quick to accept trends", the same person continues. "We are very open to new ideas and to new things." When a Swede buys clothes or a car, he or she may well be making a statement, but rarely indulges in conspicuous or ostentatious spending the way a Düsseldorfer or a Milanese might. This in no way prevents him or her from being every bit as stylish as an Austrian.

The Swedes are also an almost depressingly healthy race, despite foreign media reports of mass outbreaks of Seasonal Affective Disease (SAD) in the darker days of the year. Their long winter months may also help explain the Swedes' affinity with light, particularly the folkloric little flames of candles.

Light, in one form or another, has a symbolic role on many occasions: the candles of the Santa Lucia festival, the cemetery lanterns on All Saints' Day, the Advent Sunday candles, the *ljusstake* candelabra visible in almost every window during the Christmas season. Candles are a sign of welcome outside cafés and private houses when a party's on. In some of the more desolate parts of the country a light is left burning in the front window of every house simply as a signal to the traveller. Hardly surprising, then, that the Swedes are the largest consumers of candles in Europe!

Tradition, unlike the traditions of many other European cultures, evolves side-by-side with Swedish society. Some of the light-related rituals are of fairly recent introduction. Many of the old rural traditions disappeared along with the village communities that harboured them at the time of the 19th-century land reforms. Those that survived have become to some extent stylised. Åke Daun comments that "tradition as such has no intrinsic value for us. It has to prove its usefulness."

With the help of the country's beauty and these traditions, young or old, the Swedes counter the stereotype of seriousness with a friendly and welcoming attitude towards foreigners. Opinion polls conducted by Next Stop Sweden, the national travel and tourism council, consistently show that visitors give the Swedes a high rating for hospitality. They are described as 'open, extrovert and friendly' (some people would argue with the 'extrovert' bit).

Foreigners are impressed by the freedom of movement and right of access the country offers: no 'private property - keep out' signs. Highest ratings for friendliness and hospitality, including towards children, are awarded by visitors from Britain, Germany and Switzerland. Unsurprisingly, the Danes, Dutch, Italian and French are less impressed.

Despite their quirks, the Swedes are less complex than the Austrians. But, if anything, they are more difficult to understand. If we take the example of the Irish lady who thought the Austrians were like onions, we might say that the Swedes resemble a lightly boiled egg: a thin but brittle shell surrounding a soft and warm interior. Swedish shyness conceals a lot of human qualities: decency, concern and, yes!, even a sense of humour.

It is often said that creating empathy with a Swede is like trying to empty a ketchup bottle. At first nothing happens, then, all of a sudden, the contents splurt out all over the place (in the case of the Finns you first have to work out how to remove the cap). As somebody said, with typical Swedish understatement, "Swedes don't chat very much in bars with strangers." Also Swedes don't say "hello" to one another in hotel elevators, but may be persuaded to do so when they know there are foreigners in the hotel.

Coldness and consensus

Professor Hofstede's research (see page 46) gave the Swedes the lowest rating of all European countries on the masculinity/femininity scale, ie both sexes espoused feminine values like caring and consensus. Indeed the sex roles are less strict in Swedish society than elsewhere, the main aim of a couple being to achieve a close union and relationship.

At the same time, some foreign observers see a difference in gender attitudes. Jean Phillips-Martinsson frequently heard the comment from visiting business people that "Swedish women are warm, but the men are cold." Yet it is not the Swedish way to hug and kiss or even use terms of endearment a lot, even within the family.

Professor Daun makes the point that "Swedes find it difficult to console for example a workmate who has lost a close relative. Instead, 'consideration' is shown by keeping a distance or by acting as if nothing had happened." So the best recognition a frustrated foreigner may be entitled to is a warm commendation in an after-dinner speech.

This apparent coldness is, more often than not, a matter of shyness. Swedes try to explain this in terms of their environment. "We live in a land almost as big as France, yet we are less than nine million people", is one explanation. "Our problem is the transition from rural to urban life... Our manners are inherited from the land, we do not have the urban tradition" is another.

For the same reasons, 'coldness' cohabited with consensus. In the words of a leading Swedish industrialist, "if you couldn't choose anything but your own community, you learned the art of living together. The only exceptions to this rule were the village fool and the artist."

Both nature and history have taught Swedes to value their personal independence, despite the environment of a consensus-oriented society. People are cautious about establishing relationships and, as they see it, committing themselves. This pops up in telling little habits, like buying a cigarette off a colleague at work, or taking your own sheets when you are staying with friends.

Åke Daun identifies a curious inner tension within the Swedish psyche: "Swedes seem to need social autonomy strongly and not be dependent on other individuals, such as neighbours, employers and so on. At the same time, Swedes seem to need collective support for their opinions."

"Modernism and social engineering have complicated things for us," he continues. "We have no real roots yet in our society, we have to call in the experts. We still tend to look upwards for support and guidance. We don't yet have enough self-reliance."

A Swedish film producer who has lived a long time in France says, "where two Frenchmen will do anything to disagree, two Swedes will do anything to agree." For one thing, unlike the French, Swedes get little pleasure from talking for its own sake. For another, they only feel comfortable if they are *sams* (in agreement) with the person they are talking to. If they get to the point where they are *osams* (in disagreement), they may even break off the conversation. Conflict is unwelcome.

A Swede will quite often 'play possum' when his or her opinion is openly challenged by someone else. The laid-back instinct, a natural tendency to underplay issues, can be the cause of many misunderstandings with foreigners and is easily and falsely interpreted as indifference.

This was exemplified by the fuss over the first performance before the European Parliament of the new Swedish EU Commissioner, Anita Gradin. Confronted with a question to which she did not have the answer, she confessed "I don't know". Responding to other questions she, being a Swede, declined to answer with ten words where one would do. And instead of recognising her succinctness, the European Parliamentarians dismissed her as "vague".

This apparently low-key attitude that is so common in Swedes goes under the label of *lagom är bäst* - a phrase that in effect means "not too much, not too little, but just right!". It explains the apparent lack of national pride, the world of sports excepted - though there is a strong sense of national self-esteem, based on what is perceived as the admirable modernity of Swedish society, and a growing interest in the question of what constitutes 'Swedishness'.

It also helps explain what foreigners perceive as indecisiveness. There is an inbuilt tendency to forgo judgment, to give the other party the benefit of the doubt. The Swedish sense of democracy is expressed in this willingness to respect the other person's point of view.

Evidence of this is provided by a diary entry by Tage Erlander, Sweden's great prime minister who led the country for 23 years, quoted in Olof Ruin's biography: "I remember that already as a child I became accustomed to the fact that, when a person who was badly spoken of had the opportunity to talk about his motives, the picture was different from the one you had heard before... There must be a motive for even the most foolish act; there must be two sides to every question - therein lies the root of indecisiveness." Therein also lies the root of fairness.

In fact, Swedes consider emotional discipline to be an expression of both their humanity and their civilisation. This even extends to not drawing attention to oneself in public by talking loudly or behaving erratically.

Related to this is a reluctance - though not as marked as in the case of the Finns - to open one's mouth and put one's foot in it. Åke Daun comments that "most Swedes' lack of experience in speaking loudly in public places helps to explain why an audience so unwillingly says anything in the discussion period following a lecture... Swedes appear to reflect more than many other nationalities on how others will react to what they are saying, about what is then suitable for them to say in each and every situation, what impression they are making on others, etc... Many Swedes' relatively slow speech and numerous pauses in their speech can be explained by the importance placed on words - the fear of saying 'something rash'."

Closely related to this is the strong Swedish ethic of honesty - being honest both in what one thinks and what one says. There is a tendency to tell the truth in a very precise way. A European Values System study conducted in the early-1980s showed that 60 per cent of Swedish respondents considered lying "a bad thing". The figure for Norway was 38 per cent, for Finland 22 per cent and for Danes 13 per cent!

Worship of nature

Perhaps the most striking feature of the Swedish psyche - shared by the country's Nordic neighbours - is the affinity with nature (see box, page 144). A bright bowl of flowers is a common feature of Swedish front windows. Many Swedes spend their weekends walking or skiing through the forest, communing with the spirits and reflecting on life and its meaning. One in every two Swedes has a *stuga*, a summer house.

This affinity is hardly surprising, since nature is very close and often distinctively beautiful. Much of southern and central Sweden resembles an oversize rock garden interspersed with graceful juniper bushes and stands of oak and silver birch, all enhanced by the occasional little red house with its latticework fencing.

The Swedes have an almost religious relationship to nature. Worship is made easy by virtue of the right of common access - 'Everyman's Right' - which allows anyone to roam more or less where he or she wants in the countryside. An unwritten and inviolable right rather than a legally enacted one, it reflects a degree of respect for other people's property that you would have difficulty in finding in many other countries. It is also, together with the right to inspect official mail, the only condition absolutely insisted on in Swedish negotiations for entry to the European Union.

This affinity with nature is bred early in the average Swede. There are many allusions to the carefree days of childhood, both in personal memories and in the popular folklore of adventurous characters like Nils Holgersson, Kalle Blomkvist and, most famous of all, Pippi Longstocking whose creator, Astrid Lindgren, maintained that a happy childhood was a prerequisite for creating a better world.

Looking back, one is astonished at the difference in lifestyles of the older generations: in the big cities, it is hard to avoid running into a special race of Swedish *grandes dames* wearing startling hats as statements of some kind or another.

It's not that long ago that some of them could be seen drunk in the streets.

Looking ahead, one sees less and less evidence of a generation gap. Parent/child relationships are close, particularly in younger middle-class families. Parents are very even-handed in their treatment of children, allowing them the right to their own opinions and preferences. They participate with them actively in developing their sense of curiosity and discovery. Incidentally, it comes as a surprise to many foreigners to learn that Sweden now has one of the highest reproduction rates in Europe, twice that of Italy or Spain.

By contrast, and contrary to what many foreigners might expect, old and handicapped people are encouraged - and prefer - to live on their own. Yet the percentage of the population active in voluntary work is higher than in any other European nation.

As with the Austrians, there is an element of formalism in Swedish behaviour, even if informality is the flavour of the culture today (the Swedes used to be even more formal and reserved). But whereas with the Austrians, formalism tends to concentrate on the use of titles and similar obeisances, with the Swedes it emerges in social rather than professional encounters.

It is most evident in the speech *[tack-talet]* offered to the hostess by the guest of honour at a perfectly humdrum dinner and, even more, in the habit of saying *'tack för senaste'* ['thanks for the last time'] when being invited for the second (or third) time round. Maybe this reflects surprise at being invited for the second (or third) time round.

The polite form of address, *ni* (the equivalent of *Sie* in German), was abandoned by most people in the 60s for *du*, but is now making something of a comeback. Egalitarianism has its limits!

Like all European cultures, the Swedish culture harbours internal contradictions. "I have never met a people so prone to self-criticism, and yet so nationalistic as the Swedes", says an Englishwoman married to a Swede (maybe she should have said 'conscious of their otherness' rather than 'nationalistic').

"The Swedes are very self-focussed", says a Dane. "They have a highly developed culture and they think highly of it. This tends to make them hypercritical towards other cultures. If you find someone complaining about the bill in an international business hotel, as likely as not it's a Swede." So they're both self-critical and hypercritical about others, all at the same time? Indeed they are.

Another contradiction is the Swedish sense of democracy cohabiting with the demon of jealousy, *den kungliga svenska avundsjukan* or 'royal Swedish sickness' as it is known. Jealousy, it has to be said though, is most evident in small-town and rural life - as it is, for example, in Norway and Denmark (prompting Axel Sandemose's *'Law of Jante'*, which insists that no one should consider himself better than anyone else), as well as in the Netherlands and even in Spain *(el vicio español)*.

An inevitable feature of such a highly structured society is a killjoy element which has to be viewed in context. One is surrounded by strictures like "no strong beer before 12" and "no smoking after 2". Swedes are not averse to finding ways around such Lutheran hangups, for example by taking to Baltic steamers and drinking and smoking themselves silly. Accession to the European Union affords some relief: the *Systembolaget* drinks stores no longer have an absolute monopoly on Swedish soil. Many harrowing tales are told about standing in queue - with a ticket of course! - on a Friday evening to stock up for a boozy weekend.

The Swedes - with some notable exceptions like ice-hockey hooligans and some of the more bucolic members of the tribe - are naturally reticent in establishing relationships. They tend to husband their friendships, keeping intimacy to a narrow circle of family and close friends. No one, least of all Swedes, will deny that alcohol can help ease the process of socialising, but that would be an oversimplification of their occasionally overwheening fondness for the demon drink.

As in most other countries of the so-called 'Slav-Akvavit Belt', there is a ritual attached to the business of drinking. In their case, a tradition of drinking songs evolved over the course of the 19th century, encouraged by the emergence of student guilds and male voice choirs. Lutheran inhibitions were progressively sublimated as the repertoire of lively, yet often self-conscious, songs and ditties grew ever larger.

A Swedish doctor specialising in the treatment of alcoholism says that "the Swedes do not have an alcohol problem as much as they have a problematic relationship to alcohol. When they drink, they do so chiefly to get drunk."

Professor Daun goes further: "It has been thought that alcoholism in Sweden serves the theoretically interesting function of legitimising behaviour which would otherwise be considered culturally unacceptable - that is, the type of behaviour which goes directly against what I have so far described as being typically Swedish - silence, seriousness, avoiding conflict and strong emotions, and oriented towards the rational. Even after an insignificant amount of alcohol, Swedes have the 'right' to act boisterously and joke more than usual, to become aggressive and emotional - cry and even use emotional arguments - without risking making fools of themselves."

A large country

If you were to put a pin in the southernmost tip of Sweden and swing the country around on its axis on the map of Europe, the northernmost tip would be on a parallel with Rome.

It's a large country and, with a total population of only 8.7 million spread over a surface of 450,000 km^2 (175,000 square miles), there's room for regional variations. Moreover these local cultures are reinforced by the various dialects of Swedish, which vary substantially from province to province, and by a growing awareness of regional traditions.

As in so many other European countries, but for different reasons, the people in the north tend to look down on the people in the capital, whom they regard in the first instance as bureaucratic dissipators of the money they work so hard to earn.

Stockholm happens to be in the middle of the country so, in this case, the people of the industrial south also look up at the capital for much the same reasons.

The people in Stockholm tend to make jokes about the Gothenburgers - something to do with a couple called Karl and Ada, and a side-character with the unlikely name of Osborn - though the Gothenburgers have a reputation, even with the Stockholmers, for being witty and cosmopolitan but also very conservative. And everyone makes jokes about the krona-pinching people of Småland province.

In the words of a senior government official, "when you live in the north, you tend to look with suspicion at Stockholm. You equate the city with narcotics, criminality and politicians in that order" (though, as already said, Swedish politicians generally get a high rating for decency and for acting in the public interest). "People tend to think that, when Stockholmers come up-country, they either come as holiday-makers to get drunk or as businessmen to plunder natural resources."

The street culture of Stockholm, catalysed by increasing joblessness, is something that worries many influential people. A film producer makes the point that, whereas any conflicts used to be conflicts of interest, they are now increasingly unmotivated. Violence for violence's sake.

An article in late-1994 in *Dagens Nyheter*, the leading daily newspaper, featured the difference between a Friday night in Sveg, a small town in the Härjedalen region up north, and a Friday night in a central Stockholm area. The reporter paid visits to a police station and a hospital in both locations.

When the reporter arrived at the Sveg police station, the patrols were out verifying the whereabouts of the reindeer, just in case they strayed too close to the roads. Later that evening they were breathalysing snowscooter drivers: almost everyone makes their own *brännvin* schnapps in pot stills in the region.

A visit to the Sveg clinic produced nothing more alarming than a couple of young men with bloody heads and black eyes. When asked by a policemen if they wanted to bring charges, they retorted that "nobody ever died from a fair fight."

By contrast the scene the following Friday at the Stockholm police station was like Chicago at the height of Prohibition, while the hospital was awash with blood from knife wounds and the like. But frightened foreigners should remember that 44 per cent of Swedes live in communities of less than 10,000 people, like Sveg.

The inhabitants of the industrial and mercantile cities of the Swedish south are, again, different from the people of Stockholm. Malmö, for example, has a Hanseatic culture. A Stockholmer speaks of the south generally as having "a Harley-Davidson and Hell's Angels culture", which he claims it shares with the Danes. Another type of culture is evident in the one-company towns like Karlstad and Falun.

142

Two distinct cultures are to be found in the regions of Småland and Dalarna. Småland is remarkable for its rugged geography and remote settlements. It was the region travellers feared most on their journey from the Continent to Stockholm.

This fierce and challenging region has generated a dogged self-sufficiency in its people. Respect for money and the virtues of cooperation at the community level, including lights in farmhouse windows, go hand-in-hand with the competitive spirit - which does not preclude subcontracting work to a local competitor. The result is, among other things, a vigorous small business culture. People speak of the *Gnosjö-mopeds*, the Mercedes-Benz' of the typical factory owner of the area and the only concession to snobbery. The boss will be there on Sunday singing in the church choir, conducted by one of his workers.

Further north lies Dalarna, the land of the little red horses and the sentimental heart of the country. The national attachment to this area and its traditions reflects the fact that some of its communities survived the effects of the 18th and 19th-century land reforms.

At the northern tip of the country lies Sweden's most distinctive culture: the Sami people, still known to many foreigners as Lapps, a word that the Sami consider derogatory. Out of a total of 50-60,000 people spread across Norway, Sweden, Finland and the Kola Peninsula of Russia, 17,000 Sami are now permanently established in Sweden. Of these, 3,000 are directly dependent on reindeer breeding and culling. Despite their distinct culture and language - a series of dialects from the Finno-Ugric family - most Sami now live like other Nordics.

One thing all Lapps seem to be united on is a dislike for the people further south. In the words of one of them, speaking of the Stockholm establishment, "they have felt free to take our resources from us but, when we want to develop them ourselves, they say: 'Savages, you don't know anything about business!'."

This dislike extends to Brussels and beyond. Almost all Samis - along with *bandy* supporters - voted against accession to the European Union. Swedish Samis even contemplated secession and union with Norway.

Yet another and less-known ethnic minority, a community of Finnish-speaking Swedes, lives in the Tornedalen region on the northernmost shores of the Gulf of Bothnia.

Despite these regional differences it has to be remembered that, in the final analysis, Sweden is a relatively homogeneous society when compared with the other member states of the Union. And one factor above all others unites Swedes: their innate sense of democracy.

'Humble Spirit'

A key element in the mental makeup of the Swede, as of all Nordics, is his or her affinity to nature. John Harper of the University of Sussex examines this aspect in a case history involving a Swedish company which expressed its philosophy in a slogan that translated into English as 'Humble Spirit'.

Apart from finding the whole idea hilarious, the company's British employees had difficulty in equating humility with what they saw as the high-handed, even arrogant, manner of their Swedish bosses. Shyness, hesitation in response, a tendency to avert one's gaze are common features of Swedish behaviour and tend to be incorrectly interpreted by foreigners as arrogance.

It required insight into the Swedish mind to understand the real meaning of this company's corporate philosophy.

In John Harper's words, "for Sweden, the national environment is rich with beauty, with life-giving sources of energy, and is seen as good - and yet it is also perceived as dangerous and life-threatening. Harsh weather conditions, famines and poverty have been part of Sweden's 'bad' experiences of their natural environment. Swedish culture lays great stress on harmony, beauty, consensus, humbleness and simplicity. They can all be described as part of the Swedish respect for the 'spiritual' power of nature.

"How to reconcile a respectful attitude towards the natural environment, whilst at the same time exploiting its wealth for economic gain, proves a dilemma facing all Swedish production companies. One way of resolving this apparent conflict of values is to place a high value on the notion that anything that is extracted from the natural world, eg from trees, water, plants, ore etc and exploited by man for gain must be given the best treatment, in terms of quality, safety and beauty in order to show humble respect for the spirit of nature.

"Thus, by this analysis, *humble* means being respectful of nature, and being in harmony with the natural order and achieving this by showing a continuous *spirit* of technical excellence, betterment and aesthetic beauty. 'Humble Spirit' requires company personnel to produce high-quality products, which are technically excellent and pleasing to the eye, and to carry out the business in a spirit of quiet respect and humbleness. All personnel should be 'ordinary' and not behave in ostentatious ways which might indicate a triumph over nature."

A corporate philosophy a Japanese company could be proud of!

John Harper, CRICCOM Paper No 7,
The Centre for Research into Cross-cultural
Organisation and Management.

Big trees, no underbrush

Sweden has always been remarkable for the fact that, as a country with only slightly more people than Austria, it has generated a family of major manufacturing corporations which are the envy of the world: ASEA, Astra, Atlas Copco, Electrolux, Ericsson, Gambro, IKEA, Saab-Scania, Sandvik, SCA, SKF, Stora, Tetra Laval, Volvo and, as a joint venture with Swiss interests, ABB. Per capita, Sweden has the highest concentration of large corporations in Europe.

'Family' is the operative word, since many of these companies are linked with a family dynasty which is synonymous with Swedish big business, the Wallenbergs. The Wallenberg group (the family prefers to call it an 'association of companies') has, in the words of one business observer, "a mystique of success".

The *Economist* estimated, in 1994, that the family's interests accounted for some 40 per cent of the Swedish stock market. The paper spoke of "a concentration of economic power unequalled in Europe." Indeed the industrial scene, below the level of big business, looks rather bleak. In the words of a banker, "what you find is that Swedish manufacturing is like its forests - there are a few big fir trees, but there's no underbrush." Yet, surprisingly, what 'underbrush' there is is often as internationally minded as the 'big trees'.

An American CEO makes the point that "the basic Swedish business strategy is accretion. Yet," he adds, "Swedish business, with certain major exceptions, traditionally runs its international groups on an essentially decentralised basis. The attitude tends to be *laissez-faire*, subject to certain basic controls." Another American, working for Stockholm's City Hall, confirms this when he says that "Swedes generally think that the best way to profit from a business is to 'own a piece of the action'."

Despite the Wallenberg motto (see box overleaf) and in keeping with the principle of transparency applied in other areas of life, Swedish business is generally far less secretive than many of the other business communities in the European Union. Swedish financial reporting is among the best in Europe.

All the major Swedish companies (Wallenberg-owned or other) class as fully fledged multinationals, some of them with over a century's experience in international markets. Ericsson had substantial interests in Russia before WWI, Atlas-Copco and Alfa-Laval were well established in the USA at the same time, even Rio de Janeiro's 'Christ' was built with Swedish cement.

Indeed Swedish industry and its foreign markets were founded on ample resources of raw materials - cement, steel, timber, pulp, etc. Engineering skills and high quality standards gave the extra impetus.

As world markets opened up to them, many emergent Swedish multinationals practised a policy of what might be called 'corporate colonialism', a phenomenon also evident in German industry - from which the Swedes at that time still tended to take the lead. Being cautious by nature, Swedish top management kept a tight hold on the reins: head office would send Swedes out on 3-5 years' tours of duty to oversee foreign operations.

This policy of rotating subsidiary managers, while it ensured good communications between fellow-Swedes and an innate understanding of shared objectives, did not necessarily contribute to operational continuity and was not always popular with local subsidiary employees. Even so it seems that the policy must have merits, since some Swedish companies -

'Esse Non Vidare'

The Wallenbergs, whose 'associated companies' are reputed to account for 40 per cent of the value of the Stockholm Stock Exchange, are discreet to say the least. The family's motto reads 'Esse Non Vidare' ['To Be, Not To Be Seen'].

Capitalism *à la Wallenberg* has been able to cohabit comfortably with successive Social Democrat governments. In the words of a leading business journalist, the latter have "found it relatively easy to deal with highly concentrated and institutionalised big business." Recent changes in the laws on voting rights have to some extent attenuated these massive concentrations of power.

The Wallenberg group counts 11 of Sweden's top 15 exporters. It has invested heavily abroad in recent years and, through various channels including its Investor holding company, now rates as the second largest industrial group in Italy, without most Italians being even aware of the fact.

"The Wallenberg dominance is very dangerous because nothing develops without competition", said a senior Swedish businessman in late-1994 to the *Financial Times*. "When things get too intertwined, it's like a group of children playing - nobody sticks their neck out except one or two leaders. That will not lead to creative solutions which Sweden needs badly at the moment." This highlights the purported Swedish aversion to risktaking.

Electrolux, Ericsson and Tetra Laval included - are still practising it.

Today, more than half of all the people in the pay of Swedish industry are employed outside the country. Moreover, in many companies, foreign turnover contributes more than 90 per cent of total sales.

Unspoiled, accessible nature

Despite its reputation as a high-cost country, Sweden is increasing in popularity as a tourist destination although, compared with Austria, it has a long way to go. The industry earned over ECU 2 billion in foreign exchange in 1994. Ten years ago, 90 per cent of Swedish winter sports fans went to the Alps, 10 per cent stayed at home. Today, the situation is reversed and Continentals, particularly the Danes, are starting to discover Swedish slopes.

But summer tourism offers the greatest potential, even though the Swedish summer is a short one. Next Stop Sweden, the tourist promotion organisation, identifies a number of trump cards. First comes nature: "our nature is very unspoiled, yet very accessible. 'Ecotourism' comes naturally." The target audience is, by definition, upmarket and not unduly cost-conscious.

The second trump card is the welcome given by ordinary people to visitors: "Sweden is a happy country, we are a happy people." Swedes, despite the impressions of Auberon Waugh and some other foreigners, really enjoy life. An international survey found that twice as many Swedes claimed to be happy as the average for Europe. They are helped in achieving this level of contentment by their strong family and community relationships, and by their traditions.

The third card is the not insignificant question these days of personal safety and convenience. Sweden features a low crime rate, an excellent health service and a warm and imaginative reception for families with children. Cuisine is simple and tasty.

Sweden does not have the same symbiotic relationship between tourism and agriculture as Austria. With progressive rationalisation, both through the country's history and since 1991, the farming industry has become increasingly concentrated. Moreover only eight per cent of Swedish land is arable, 52 per cent is forest and the rest is urban, mountain or marshland. Today, less than two per cent of the working population is engaged in agriculture, including forestry.

Of the 90,000 farm units left in this huge country, two-thirds are still managed and worked by part-time farmers. Most of these grow cereals or keep sheep. These part-time farmers generally find alternative employment in industry, with 'mechanical workshops' *[mekaniska verkstäderna]* and other manufacturing operations in most towns of any size. Of the full-time farms, two-thirds are engaged in dairy farming with an average of 25 cows.

The average Swedish farm has 30 hectares of arable land and some 50 hectares of forest. There are only 4,000 estates of more than 100 hectares, of which 1,000 in the southernmost province of Skåne, the rest mainly in the Lake Mälaren area.

Consensus and compromise

As with Swedish society, the leitmotiv of Swedish industry is the principle of consensus. What many foreigners would perceive as an exaggerated process of consultation and dialogue is used to reach mutually acceptable business decisions. This does not mean there is no room for dissent. After all, as a Swedish businessman says, "if everyone thought like the boss, there wouldn't be much thinking..."

A worthy principle, consensus is not always evident in practice. One of Sweden's top business journalists considers that the institution of the two-tier board system, with blue-collar representatives on the supervisory board, is essentially "window dressing". He insists however that co-determination is more evolved than in other European countries. Moreover compromise is in no sense regarded as a sign of weakness in Swedish eyes.

A Swedish management expert asserts that, whatever the appearances, many of the most important decisions are still made "up in the clouds" at boardroom level, before the consensus process starts. He also says that people running foreign subsidiaries often complain to him about the difficulties of getting through to Swedish top management. "There's an Old Boys' Network and, if you're out, you're out!"

The same person comments that, when decisions are taken by a group, there can be a mutual conspiracy to avoid identifying anybody in particular with the decision, in case something goes wrong. "You don't openly commit yourself, you leave yourself room to deny your responsibility, you make sure you have some alibis." Opinions are more suggestive than decisive.

But it is also part of the conspiracy that, if something does indeed go wrong, the 'passengers' avoid pointing fingers at the luckless individual who is perceived as the 'driver'. And there is rarely a postmortem. In the words of a Swedish businessman who has close contacts with France: "If something goes wrong, Swedes will immediately form a group to find a solution. The French will find a scapegoat."

This may sound aberrant to people steeped in either Anglo-Saxon or autocratic (eg French) management styles, but it somehow fits the Swedish psyche. In her book 'Swedes as Others see Them', Jean Phillips-Martinsson speaks about "the lack of a spirit of adventure, the fear to take risks, over-cautiousness and delay in taking decisions and meeting delivery deadlines..."

Many people comment that Swedish managers prefer to stick to proven methods rather than take chances. "They don't make decisions fast", comments the American CEO, "they're simply not natural gamblers. Sometimes they also factor social issues into their reasoning." The business journalist referred to earlier also makes the point that managers of Swedish foreign subsidiaries, who expect quick and effective head office decisions, rarely get them.

As cautious people, the Swedes show a natural reluctance to invite risk unless it is essential to the proper running of a business, as in the case of long-term capital investments in the engineering industry. In this respect, Swedes stand on a scale close to the Germans and mid-point between the Americans on the one hand and the Japanese on the other.

Both stock market and blue-collar union attitudes favour the principle of long-term industrial growth. While these attitudes are reflected in a conciliatory mood towards big corporations, they unfortunately mean a lack of support for the young entrepreneur starting his own business. Evoking the image offered by the banker, in the absence of any significant venture capital initiatives, little is being done to create an industrial "underbrush".

Even so, Sweden's management schools are generating a growing reserve of young talent - in particular Stockholm's Handelshögskolan (sponsored by the Wallenbergs), Gothenburg University, Uppsala University, the Jönköping International Business School and the Swedish Institute of Management (IFL). The Handelshögskolan is the breeding ground for the Old Boys' Network mentioned earlier.

Much of this young talent is already climbing the corporate ladder, with the traditional engineers making way for economists and marketing specialists. At the time of writing Leif Johansson, the CEO of Electrolux, is in his late-30s and the company's chief comptroller is only 32.

It could be that a combination of youthfulness and shyness create the impression, in the words of a close observer, that "Swedish managers tend to be a bit socially and intellectually immature." Percy Barnevik of ABB is another example of a relative youngster made good - though as the same person, showing typically Swedish scepticism, queries, "where is the real man?"

Social skills, or lack of them, crop up frequently in conversation with foreigners. A French businessman comments bluntly that "it is very difficult to make conversation with a Swede." Small talk is indeed not a strong point. But, like the French, the Swedes tend to make a clear distinction between their professional and their private lives. Swedes find it completely natural not to socialise privately with colleagues, even if they have worked together for years.

Another Frenchman who runs a Swedish subsidiary comments that "my Swedish colleagues strike me as being very cold and matter-of-fact. I tell them my troubles and they say 'ja, ja' and seem to change the subject." In fact, they're not changing the subject. They've registered the problem, unemotionally, and have moved on to the next point on the agenda.

"Swedes are discreet people," comments the American CEO. "Much of what goes on is tacit   no wonder foreigners have difficulty in following them at times. Swedish management is level-headed to the point of being phlegmatic. But, if something goes wrong, they do tend to flap their wings."

Another French observer - the French coming from such an alien culture are sensitive to these things - comments that "there is a kind of shyness in a way, and aggressiveness in others, a kind of superiority complex in some cases, and inferiority complex in others." Many people comment on the shyness of the average Swede, often dissimulated behind a facade of courteousness but occasionally, when under stress, manifesting itself in an excessive self-assertiveness.

"The lack of a word for 'please' in the Swedish language", comments Jean Phillips-Martinsson, addressing the Swedish readers of her book, "means that you are inclined to exclude it even in English. This omission can well account for your reputation of being curt and giving orders." Elsewhere she makes the interesting observation that "in Swedish eyes, being honest means telling the truth and keeping your word. This means that [the Swedish businessman] is unlikely to give compliments as, in his eyes, it would be an exaggeration of the truth."

The experience of walking into a Stockholm bank and, as a naive foreigner, expecting service by standing at the counter - instead of taking a ticket and watching for a number to come up - is echoed in another of Ms Phillips-Martinsson's comments: "... the interminable waiting. Waiting to be served in the shops, in the restaurants and waiting for the bill. Not to mention the hospitals! Are these the effects of a classless society, I wondered? Those in service had an incredible knack of simply not noticing my existence, or of being much too busy chatting with one another to care."

Opinions differ on Swedish negotiating skills. One observer says that "the Swedes are very good at negotiating. They do their research, and they expect written agreements." Another says "they are not easygoing but have a stiff, hard, businesswise attitude."

Jean Phillips-Martinsson maintains, on the one hand, that the Swede "is totally inflexible in negotiations. He doesn't negotiate at all. He says 'let's discuss my proposal', but has no intention of discussing anything, his mind is made up." Yet, she insists, they can be very patient in negotiations, using silence to "digest your questions, formulate their reply and to motivate their next move..." The pretence of not properly understanding your English can be a useful technique. Silent pauses are more common in negotiations with Swedes than with Germans.

Certainly the Swedes bargain hard but almost always correctly. Like other Nordics and the British, they prefer to avoid adversarial business relationships. Quite often, foreigners are surprised to discover that the Swedish side has already agreed with what they are proposing, but hasn't bothered to say so explicitly...

Foreigners frequently comment on the apparent reluctance of Swedish managers to reply to letters. "Strange bods, the Swedes", says a British businessman: "Been dealing with them for years but they never keep in touch once a sale has been made." The truth is that, being busy and a long way off, they prefer to communicate electronically if at all. In the words of one of them, "a letter is something that is outdated." Fax and E-mail may also suit their temperament as they're less personal.

Let us leave the last words on the subject to Ms Phillips-Martinsson, who conducted an opinion poll among 171 foreign businessmen to discover how the Swedish businessman is rated in the world. "In brief", she concluded, "the Swedish businessman was regarded as inflexible in his negotiations and behaviour - unwilling to discuss and adjust, slow to make decisions, avoids conflict, over-cautious, and a stickler for punctuality. Difficult to get to know, hard to work with and for, stiff, no fun, dull and conceited."

But they're not like that really. They just have an image problem!

Postscript

Ah yes, Norway!

That the country turned EU membership down twice came as a disappointment, but not a surprise.

If we talked about the nation that 'got away' - as some people did after the narrowly negative referendum - the implication was that the 4 1/2 million Norwegians were there to be 'caught' by the European Union. This underestimates these people in several important respects.

Precisely because there was irritation with the Norwegians in Brussels after the "no" vote, it is tempting to write them off as stubborn eccentrics, laughable even. That would be simplistic.

In history, trade, defence and civilisation (Ibsen's plays, Munch paintings, Grieg's music and, most recently, Jostein Gaarder's 'Sophie's World'), Norway has long been part of Europe. As a NATO member which played a seminal part in the Middle East's diplomatic games and still has the majesterial good fortune to own vast oil and gas reserves in the North Sea, Norway can't just be regarded as a country of hairy-backed whale killers...

Indeed, it's these natural riches that have reinforced the sense of self and autonomy in post-war Norway.

The wealth is palpable - and not just because of the prices, though Norway's cost of living can drain the colour from a foreigner's face. It is evident in the poise, style and confidence of its citizens, up-country as well as in the cities.

Twenty-two years ago, we thought the Norwegians had fallen off a cliff by their rejection of the Common Market of the time. How wrong we were and, such is the character of the people, there is little evidence of hand-wringing now that the other Nordic Council members have opted for the Union.

The Norwegians' instinctive rejection of what they see as the EU's bureaucracy, conceit and secrecy has not left them feeling uneasy. They believe they have seen aspects of the Union's character that others are reluctant to acknowledge.

Despite the untidiness of Norway, and Switzerland, staying outside the EU, there is a politically wholesome lesson in their action for the rest of us.

Every media reference to the referendum's "no" makes the point that the Norwegians are different. More often than not, it's a Norwegian who's making the point.

But how different? They don't argue that they are European like the rest of us, they just happen to be obstinate in their conviction that they are special. They demonstrate a particularly strong sense of equality (a sense that the Swedes have equally, but demonstrate less), an epidermic reaction to authority from outside (brought on by submission first to Denmark and then to Sweden) and a pride in the beauty and grandiosity of their country that strikes many foreigners as a bit exaggerated.

In fact the Norwegians are just as European as the other Nordics. They are an important part of European history, having discovered Greenland (a great propaganda stunt, "green"!) and, some say, North America. More recently, they showed great courage and stubbornness in resisting the Nazis in World War II. They know, moreover, that they will never be turned down for EU membership if they apply again.

"Hey, we're just about to become non-Europeans!", joked a dandified Norwegian yuppie to his equally elegant friends as they prepared to celebrate the arrival of 1995 at the 'Hannibal's Hybel' pub on Oslo's harbour front.

A burst of laughter accompanied the clink of glasses. If it was bravado, it didn't seem like it. But even for them - proud and outside - there was a feeling that an age of innocence had passed. Life may get harder.

Certainly, the Norwegians are special - as is the country's gaunt and imposing geography.

We miss them!

About the Authors

Richard Hill is a Brussels-based writer, consultant and lecturer specialising in cross-cultural relations. He has over twenty years' experience as a consultant in pan-European communications and is the author of *"WeEuropeans"* and *"EuroManagers & Martians"*, studies of the general and business cultures of Europe. He lectures at various European and US universities and business schools.

David Haworth, also based in Brussels, is an EU public affairs consultant and journalist, who has been professionally involved with Finland for over twenty years. Formerly a spokesman for the European Commission in the US and a winner of the European Journalism Prize, Haworth has also lectured extensively on EU politics.

163

WeEuropeans

Whatever doubts we may have about Maastricht, many of us hold fervently to the idea of a united Europe. And opinion polls among the young show a growing commitment to the European ideal.

This Europe is all about people – people who differ in their tastes and habits but share the same values and ideals. Understanding them, understanding one another, is a crucial step in the process of creating a Europe where unity cohabits with diversity.

Richard Hill talks about the people in this book. He starts by describing, then attacking, the stereotypes and moves on to a witty and skilful analysis of each of the European cultures.

He then enlarges his theme with a comparative analysis of value systems and lifestyles, how people communicate, relate to one another and do business. The final chapter examines recent events and offers thoughts on where we go from here.

"...a fascinating book. His dissection of each nationality produces some wonderful sociological insights."

The European

"Richard Hill starts from the obvious to discover the difficult and makes an impressive success of it."

Emanuele Gazzo, *Agence Europe*

"A delightful and very funny book. I'll buy it!"

Derek Jameson, *BBC Radio 2*

"I can warmly recommend a wonderful book by Richard Hill, 'WeEuropeans'." **Libby Purves,** *BA High Life*

EuroManagers & Martians
Richard Hill

The Business Cultures of Europe's Trading Nations

EuroManagers & Martians

Looking at them simply as people, when we see them in the streets of Paris or when we visit them *chez eux*, our fellow-Europeans come across as a pretty odd lot – a far cry from the Single Market, harmonisation and all those dreary things.

But how do they behave in business? Put a German, a Frenchman, a Spaniard, an Italian, a Swede and, of course, a Brit together around a negotiating table and what happens? Either nothing at all – they just don't know how to deal with one another – or a lot! It's then that you realise that, despite all the constraints of working within a business environment, life à *l'européenne* is still full of surprises.

The simple fact, of course, is that it would need a super-human to leave his cultural baggage behind him simply because he puts on his coat to go to the office. This book examines the business cultures of Europe's main trading nations and offers useful insights into differences in attitudes to time, hierarchy, protocol, negotiating styles, acceptance of management disciplines and multicultural teamwork.

With so much cultural diversity even in business, the author wonders how on earth we are going to develop the Euromanager we keep hearing about, the person who is going to save us from the Japanese, the Asian Tigers and others. Will this Euro-superman-ager ever exist?

"The book is written from an alien's point of view, and it presents both carefully researched and anecdotal evidence in an entertaining read... Carefully steering a course away from the stereotype path, Hill gives well-considered and practical advice on conducting Eurobusiness."   **The European**

Have You Heard This One? An Anthology of European Jokes

An Anthology of European Jokes
in ENGLISH - in het NEDERLANDS - en FRANÇAIS - in DEUTSCH

Here are some of the better jokes we Europeans tell about one another. There are a lot of bad ones – far too many – but you will find none of them here.

Good European jokes are neither stupid nor abusive. They tell one something instructive about the way people from different cultures perceive one another. And some of these jokes shed light on the cultures of both the 'sender' and the 'receiver'.

Humour is the subtlest expression of culture, which explains why English people have difficulty in understanding German jokes. Even the psychology of humour is coloured by the attitudes of the different cultures. Yet there is common ground in European humour: some of these jokes turn up in various guises in various places.

As that eminent European Johann Wolfgang von Goethe said, rather severely: "There is nothing in which people more betray their character than in what they laugh at". Taken in the right spirit, humour is an excellent starting point for cross-cultural comprehension.

GREAT BRITAIN LITTLE ENGLAND

Britons have recently been bombarded and bludgeoned with books examining the reasons for their country's dramatic decline.

But, while offering heavily documented analyses of culprit 'constituencies' - labour, management, educators, civil servants, government itself - these books have stopped short of examining the mindsets, motivations and mannerisms common to the actors in the drama.

In this book, Richard Hill sets out to fill the gap. Starting with himself, he tries to get under the skin of the British - more specifically, the English - and understand where they go right and why they go wrong.

This is an entertaining and thought-provoking book by a Briton who has had the advantage of living outside his island culture, yet consorting closely with it, for the last 30 years.

"Wonderful stuff. Witty and accurate without being cynical."

John Mole, author of 'Mind Your Manners'

What the press says

International

"...a fascinating book. His dissection of each nationality produces some wonderful sociological insights"

The European

"Richard Hill starts from the obvious to discover the difficult and makes an impressive success of it"

Emanuele Gazzo, *Agence Europe*

"For a thorough, fundamental understanding of what makes the neighbouring natives tick, this book is a must. Vive la différence!

Eurodiagnostic

"'WeEuropeans' is a lucid, readable book which achieves that most remarkable balance: it is serious and entertaining at the same time. It contains enough hard facts, anecdotes, and examples to make its analyses persuasive. Yet never does it bog down. It is 'must' reading for anyone who seeks to work or live transnationally - and intelligently - within the Europe of the late 20th century"

Andres Garrigo, *Europe Today*

"C'est un livre qui parle, j'allais dire avec tendresse, des Européens"

Serge Flamé, *RTBF TV Belgium/TV5 Europe*

Great Britain

"A delightful and very funny book. I'll buy it!"

Derek Jameson, *BBC Radio 2*

"I can warmly recommend a wonderful book by Richard Hill, "WeEuropeans"

BA High Life

"A very European book, which I liked very much"

Manchester Evening News

"A new book called "WeEuropeans" explores the differences, but also celebrates what we have in common"

BBC Radio Scotland

168

"... a book that has been described as both serious and entertaining, and a 'must' for reading for anyone who seeks to work or live transnationally. And best of all, in my mind at least, it's got humour" **Diana Luke,** *GLR Radio, London*

"Let me commend to you his book called "WeEuropeans"... it's a fascinating read. He'll make you smile on page after page after page" **Alex Dickson,** *Radio Clyde*

"A good recipe for entertaining reading... for the pleasure of us all" *Local Government Review*

France

"Cet ouvrage très documenté propose non sans humour, au-delà des stéréotypes habituels, une analyse pertinente et percutante" *La Gazette du Tourisme*

"One of the most interesting books I've ever looked at" **Patrick Middleton,** *Riviera Radio*

"An important and needed book has been published analyzing the welter of national mentalities that comprise the Old Continent. Entitled WeEuropeans, the book is already causing wide comment and discussion" **John Van Den Bos,** *FUSAC*

Germany

"Das Buch 'Wir Europäer' des Engländers Richard Hill ist in Brüssel zum absoluten Bestseller avanciert. Mild ironisch analysiert er die Gewohnheiten der Euro-Völker, deckt Gemeinsamkeiten und Unterschiede auf, weist auf Stärken und Schwächen hin" **Birgit Svensson,** *Wochenpost*

"Wir Europäer: Zum Lachen!" *BZ am Sonntag*

Netherlands

"'WeEuropeans' hoort verplichte lectuur te zijn voor elke deelnemer aan een Eurotop. Het zou de sfeer opvrolijken en de besluitvorming versnellen. De Europeanen, binnen en buiten de EG, zouden

er wel bij varen. Om hen gaat het toch altijd, beweren de regering-sleiders onvermoeid"

Henk Aben, *Algemeen Dagblad*

"Een onderhoudend boek, dat gezien de huidige ontwikkelingen binnen de Gemeenschap niet alleen actueel, maar ook leerzaam is"

Haye Thomas, *Haagsche Courant*

"Menselijke kijk op Europa"

Het Financiëele Dagblad

"Hill wil afrekenen met de bestaande, onjuiste stereotypen en - vooral - streeft hij naar meer onderling begrip bij de volken binnen het Europese huis. Daarbij is hij niet over één nacht ijs gegaan. Tijdens zijn reizen heeft Hill allerlei eigenaardigheden en gebruiken van de Europese volken opgespoord. Zo is hij gekomen tot grappige constateringen"

Reformatorisch Dagblad

Luxembourg

"Ainsi, il détruit bon nombre de mythes et révèle la richesse et la diversité de ce monde qui fait l'Europe"

Tageblatt

"Ein insgesamt sehr unterhaltsamer, nicht ganz bierernst zu nehmender Beitrag zum Dauerthema 'Europa' - wohltuend besonders durch den Verzicht auf jegliche 'ethnocentricity' und den stets mitschwingenden humoristischen Unterton"

Letzeburger Journal

"Un livre très amusant, rédigé en anglais par un "British man in Brussels"

Euromagazine

Belgium

"Richard Hill, een in België wonende Brit, ging in zijn boek 'WeEuropeans' op zoek naar het hoe en waarom van dat tegenstrijdige Europa, naar de kloof tussen wil en daad, utopie en realiteit. Hij stuitte daarbij op vaak diepgewortelde nationale en regionale reflexen"

De Standaard Magazine

"Nous allons parler aujourd'hui d'un livre qui n'est pas écrit en français, mais en anglais, un anglais assez facile d'accès d'ailleurs pour tous ceux qui connaissent cette langue, et d'ailleurs pour ceux qui l'étudient c'est un excellent exercice"

Jean-Paul Andret, *RTL TV*

170

"De britse premier Thatcher zei ooit dat als de Europese éénwording doorgaat zoals ze bezig is alle nationale eigenschappen zullen verdwijnen en er een soort Europese éénheidsmens zal ontstaan. Onzin, vindt Hill" **Guy Janssen**, *BRT1 TV*

"Ich bin der Meinung, dass dieses Werk für Supra-National-Denkende und Supra-National-Agierende ein Muss sein sollte, analysiert es doch messerscharf sogennante Stereotypen. Mit viel Humanismus, Witz, Liebe zum Detail, Zärtlichkeit und Fachkenntnis zeigt Richard Hill uns auf gleichzeitig ernste und unterhaltsame aber auch auf überzeugende und intelligente Weise, wo die Wurzel unserer Heimat sich befindet: nämlich in einer europäischen Identität der Gleichheit in der Verschiedenheit"

Helmuth Hilgers, *BRF Radio*

"Richard Hill est anglais et pourtant il adore l'Europe... L'Europe pour lui ce n'est ni le PAC, ni la DGIII ni le paquet Delors ni même la D2 MacPacket... mais des gens, des habitudes, des tics, des différences. Une richesse formidable qui donne plutôt l'envie de rire que de pleurer ou de manifester devant le Berlaymont d'ailleurs vide. Richard Hill sait capter l'air du temps... c'est drôle, mouvementé, documenté..." **Myriam Gooris**, *Radio 21*

"Il fallait être Britannique pour oser le pari, il fallait avoir vécu longtemps à Bruxelles pour le réussir. C'est le cas de l'Anglais Richard Hill" **Violaine Muûls**, *L'Evénement*

"'We Europeans' is an excellent read on many levels, whether for the expert who is looking for new ideas to research or for those who are looking to understand their neighbours (and themselves) a little better" *AmCham*

"Même lorsqu'il égratigne légèrement l'une ou l'autre susceptibilité nationale, l'auteur ne le fait jamais méchamment car il se veut compréhensif, non dénué de tendresse et d'humour qui vous feront sourire lorsque vous vous reconnaîtrez au travers de la lecture"

Swissnews

"In his book Richard Hill addresses the differences... he says that they have reasons for existing, he just had to figure out what they were" *Radio Flanders International*

"From health to hygiene, humour to holidays, Hill leaves no stereotype unturned"   The Bulletin

"'WeEuropeans' will entertain even the best-travelled European. For those whose experience is limited to only one or two countries, it comes under the heading of essential reading"   Business Journal

"This is a book about Europeans - a description of characteristics, attitudes, hopes and habits along the continent's ethnic and national divides. More than a simple country-by-country profile of personality and prejudice, Mr Hill has attempted to root in their history and culture much of how Europeans appear to others"   Business Links

"Ik wens u veel plezier toe met uw boek "WeEuropeans", veel succes"   **Tony Van den Bosch,** BRT TV, De Zevende Dag

The Nordic Countries

"Mens velgere i stadig flere land vender seg mot sine ledere og deres store unions-dremmer; hva er mer aktuelt enn en bok som vil ta oss med på en kulturell reise i det europeiske mangfold?"
Dagbladet, Norway

"Godt er det, for Norge og nordmenn har fått en relativt mild og hederlig omtale, sammenlignet med de andre europeiske land og folk"   Aftonbladet, Norway

"Det fastslår den britiske markedsføreren og PR-mannen Richard Hill, nå ute på det norske bokmarkedet med den internasjonale bestseller 'Vi europeere'. En bok om folk og kulturer i vår mangfoldige verdensdel"   Kampanje, Norway

"I bästsäljaren 'We Europeans' finns vi redan med på ett hörn, som ett hyggligt men gammaldags folk med dörrar som öppnas utåt... 'We Europeans', en munter och innehållsrik bok som snabbt blivit populär bland EG-folket"   Dagens Nyheter, Sweden

"Hill mainitsee sivumennen myös, että suomalaiset juovat paljon. Tämäkin mielikuvaongelma jälleen kerran! Lukiessa eteenpäin käy ilmi, että hän tarkoittaa maidon kulutusta"   Turun Sanomat, Finland

'WeEuropeans', 'EuroManagers & Martians' and other Europublic books have been selected as course material by the following institutions:

BELGIUM
Antwerp University (UFSIA), English Dept.
Erasmus Hogeschool, Brussels
European University, Brussels/Antwerp
Gent University, Department of Sociology
Hoge Technische Instituut, Brugge
ICHEC Business School, Brussels
Institut für Erwachsenenbildung, Eupen/St Vith
ISC Saint-Louis Business School, Brussels
KUL Leuven
KVH Interpreters School, Antwerp
Solvay Business School (ULB), MEB Programme
United Business Institutes, Brussels
Université de Mons, Sciences Economiques

BRITAIN
Institute of Management (IM)
The Centre for International Briefing
The Open University

DENMARK
Copenhagen Business High School

FINLAND
Helsinki Institute
Jyväskylä University, European Studies
Vaasa University, European Studies

FRANCE
Groupe ESC, Lyon
INSEAD, Fontainebleau
Université de Nancy II

GERMANY
Hochschule der Künste, Berlin
Mercator Universität, Duisburg

NETHERLANDS
HEAO business course
Netherlands Institute for MBA Studies, Utrecht
Nijenrode University, Breukelen

SWEDEN
Swedish Institute of Management (IFL)
University of Lund

USA
Antioch University, Ohio
Chicago University, Graduate School of Business
Massachusetts University (Plymouth)
Michigan State University
New York University, Stern School of Business
Temple University School of Business and
    Management, Philadelphia
UCI Graduate School of Management, Irvine (CA)
University of Pennyslvania

and the training arms of various international corporations.

Services Available

Europublic represents the authors of this book, Richard Hill and David Haworth, as well as other specialists in European affairs.

In addition to book publishing, Europublic provides speakers on cross-cultural topics and conducts tailored in-company training courses on cultural issues impacting on organisations operating in an international and multicultural environment.

In addition to lecturing at various European and US universities and business schools, Europublic specialists act as speakers and consultants with various organisations in both the public and private sectors. These include the European Commission, the Helsinki Institute, the 'Eurochannels' conference organisation, Citibank, GE Capital, the IBM International Education Centre, Medtronic, Pioneer, Price Waterhouse and 3Com Europe.

For further information on these services, please mail or fax to:

Europublic SA/NV
Avenue W. Churchill 11 (box 21)
B - 1180 Brussels
Tel: +32-2-343.77.26
Fax: +32-2-343.93.30

O **WeEuropeans** (expanded edition)
ISBN 90-74440-05-3

| BF 700 | HFl 38,50 | FF 115,- | £13.99 | DM 39,90 | AS 215,- | SFr 29,90 |

O **EuroManagers & Martians**
ISBN 90-74440-02-9

| BF 695,- | HFl 38,50 | FF 115,- | £12.99 | DM 39,90 | AS 215,- | SFr 29,90 |

O **Have You Heard This One?**
An Anthology of European Jokes
ISBN 90-74440-03-7

| BF 195,- | HFl 9,95 | FF 33,50 | £ 3.99 | DM 12,90 | AS 65,- | SFr 6,95 |

O **Great Britain, Little England**
ISBN 90-74440-04-5

| BF 495,- | HFl 25,00 | FF 80,- | £ 9.99 | DM 29,90 | AS165,- | SFr 24,90 |

O **The NewComers**
ISBN 90-74440-06-1

| BF 595,- | HFl 29,90 | FF 90,- | £ 10,99 | DM 34,- | AS 195,- | SFr 28,50 |

Other books on European cultures are in preparation.

If you have difficulty in obtaining any of these books through your local bookstore, you can order from the publisher,
Europublic SA/NV,
Avenue Winston Churchill 11 (box 21), B-1180 Brussels
Tel. +32-2-343.77.26 - Fax +32 2-343.93.30

Name: ....

Address:..

....

....

Tel: .... Fax: ....